$
Home-
(Full or Part-time)

Starting a
Home-Based Business
(Full or Part-time)

Irene Korn
and
Bill Zanker

A Citadel Press Book
Published by Carol Publishing Group

Carol Publishing Group Edition, 1995

A Citadel Press Book
Published by Carol Publishing Group
Citadel Press is a registered trademark of Carol Communications, Inc.

Editorial Offices: 600 Madison Avenue, New York, NY 10022
Sales & Distribution Offices: 120 Enterprise Avenue, Secaucus, NJ 07094
In Canada: Canadian Manda Group, One Atlantic Avenue, Suite 105
Toronto, Ontario, M6K 3E7

Queries regarding rights and permissions should be addressed to:
Carol Publishing Group, 600 Madison Avenue, New York, NY 10022

Manufactured in the United States of America
10 9 8 7 6 5 4 3 2

Carol Publishing Group books are available at special discounts
for bulk purchases, sales promotions, fund raising, or
educational purposes. Special editions can also be created to
specifications. For details contact: Special Sales Department,
Carol Publishing Group, 120 Enterprise Ave., Secaucus, NJ 07094

Library of Congress Cataloging-in-Publication Data

Korn, Irene.
    Starting a home-based business (full or part-time) by Irene Korn
and Bill Zanker.
        p. cm.
    "The Learning Series Book."
    "A Citadel Press Book."
    ISBN 0-8065-1472-8
    1. Self-employed—Handbooks, manuals, etc. 2. New business
enterprises—Management—Handbooks, manuals, etc. 3. Small
business—Management—Handbooks, manuals, etc. 4. Part-time
employment—Handbooks, manuals, etc. 5. Supplementary employment—
Handbooks, manuals, etc. I. Zanker, Bill. II. Title.
HD8036.K67   1993
658'.071—dc20   93-11589
                                                              CIP

Contents

Introduction

Work in your own home. *Be your own boss. Set your own hours. Do work that you love. Make lots of money.*

Sounds great, doesn't it? And for many people, starting a home-based business of their own really does provide all that...and much more. For others, though, it can be difficult, frustrating, and expensive. What's the difference between those who succeed and those who don't?

We've all had it drilled into our heads that we can do whatever we want—as long as we want it badly enough and are willing to work for it. True—desire, hard work, and commitment are usually necessary to make a business a success, but they are only part of the equation. Plenty of hard-working people aren't able to make a go of their businesses, while for others, everything just seems to fall into place. How do you know if you can do it?

There's no one specific profile of the kind of person who succeeds in a home-based business. Owners include men and women, singles and married people, college educated and not—in other words, *all* kinds of people.

Some are twenty-somethings disillusioned with working for other people. Others are thirty-somethings who want to spend more time with their children. Then there are the forty-somethings who haven't gone as far in their careers as they had hoped. And the fifty-somethings who are tired of having to listen to people with less experience than they.

And, finally, the sixty-and-over-somethings who want a chance to finally do what they really love.

The one thing they all have in common is that they are part of a fast-growing trend. According to studies by Link Resources Corporation, a New York-based research and consulting firm, the number of part- and full-time self-employed home workers reached almost twenty-four million in 1992. By 1995, the number of people who do all or part of their work from their homes (including telecommuters and after-hours corporate workers) is expected to make up a full one-third of the adult working population.

As the numbers grow, so do the numbers of people ready to tell you the correct way to start your home-based business. But there is no one right way. What works for one person starting one kind of business will not necessarily work for another setting up a different kind of business. This book was written as a guide to the various "real" ways of starting and running your business, rather than the "right" ways.

Starting A Home-Based Business (Full or Part-time) is based on the experiences of all kinds of people—with a variety of backgrounds, needs, desires, and goals—as well as on our own very different experiences in starting our own businesses. Irene Korn started her home-based writing and editing business mostly because she had a strong desire to be her own boss, to choose her own projects, and to work hours that fit her own natural rhythm, which didn't generally coincide with the traditional nine-to-five routine. At the moment, she has no intention of ever moving her office out of her home.

Bill Zanker, on the other hand, moved out of his home office after only one year. In 1980, he started The Learning Annex, an adult education school, with $2,000 saved from his bar mitzvah money. His father had laid down the law and told him it was time he stopped being a student and started supporting himself. But Bill loved being a student and took a chance that a lot of other people would, too.

His hunch was right on the money: Within a couple of years, The Learning Annex had become a multimillion-dollar company with offices nationwide. Bill is currently heading up their venture into cable TV (scheduled to take off in 1994), in order to offer seminars to people who can't go out to take them.

Whether you already have a business concept or are just playing around with the idea of starting your own business, this book will help you decide if a home-based business is really for you, define your goals, and take you step-by-step through the process of actually starting and running your business. Good luck!

Starting a
Home-Based Business
(Full or Part-time)

1 | *Making the Decision*

 $\mathbf{T}$ hink about the last time you accepted a full-time (or even part-time) job. The scenario probably went something like this: You heard about the job (through the paper, a friend, employment agency) and thought it sounded like something you might be interested in. After you sent in your resumé, company employees also decided they might be interested in you and asked you to come in for an interview. During the interview process, you were asked questions to see how closely your skills, experience, and personality fit with what they needed. You made sure to find out exactly what the job involved, what hours you would be expected to work, your salary, benefits, and so on.

The company decided you could provide them with something they needed and offered you the job. Before you accepted, you considered all the information you had gathered, compared the new job to your old in terms of advantages and disadvantages, and decided it was to your benefit to take the job.

You wouldn't have dreamed of taking the job without knowing your salary, would you? Of course not. Even people who work on straight commission estimate what they expect to make; hourly workers multiply their salary by their likely hours to get an idea of their weekly paychecks. Depending on your own personal priorities, you would give more or less consideration to the other factors involved, but at the least you would think about: work hours, distance from home, prestige of the company, potential to move up, security, opportunity to learn, financial benefits like insurance and retirement plans, less tangible benefits like vacation time, flex time, and so on.

When you're planning your own business, you'll need to consider all the same factors you would think about when taking any other new job. Granted, some people just cross their fingers, jump in, and hope for the best. And sometimes this approach works. Most of us, however, would rather have at least some idea of what to expect.

Advantages of a Home Office

Following are some of the advantages most often cited by home-business owners. Read them carefully. In many cases, an advantage can be a disadvantage at the same time. (For example, as the owner of your own business, you're in charge, with no boss to give you orders. Sounds great. But that's only half of the equation; the flip side is you're also completely responsible. You have no one to blame for anything. When you look at it that way, it can also be a little scary.)

- *Flexibility* You can decide your work days and number of hours, the times you actually work, the assignments or orders you want to accept, and your work flow—to some degree. But you will still have some constraints, most often connected to money. You might find that you want to tell an annoying client to get lost, but you can't because you need the money. Maybe you can work all night and sleep all day if you want to. Or maybe you can't—if you're making sales calls, for example, you'll need to do them during normal working hours.

- *Low overhead* Working from home is generally quite a bit cheaper than setting up an outside office, but it's not free by any means. You'll still need to pay for equipment, supplies, utilities, and so on.
- *Reduced living expenses* If you're leaving a full-time job, you'll probably find that you end up saving money on a lot of small items. What do you think you used to spend on transportation, lunches, dry cleaning, work clothes, your morning snack, impulse buys on the way to and from work? Of course, not everyone will be able to eliminate all of these costs—and you might find yourself adding new ones—but items like these can add up to a lot of money.
- *Variety* You'll probably find yourself interacting with a variety of different people and performing many different kinds of functions. If you've been feeling bored or stifled, this kind of opportunity can be exciting. Realistically, though, there's a good chance you won't like *all* the different things you have to do as part of owning your own business.
- *Children* Be wary of this one! Many people decide to work at home either to save on day-care expenses or to be able to spend more time with their children. Working from home does offer more flexibility, but most home-business owners quickly realize how difficult it is to achieve anything when they're trying to work and watch the children at the same time.

Other advantages of a home office include no commuting time, no office politics, no slow decision-making process or hierarchy, and no staff meetings.

Disadvantages of a Home Office

Now for some of the kinds of problems that home-based·
business owners *can* encounter. Methods of dealing with
these are offered in the following chapters.

- Isolation
- Loss of privacy
- Slow business growth
- Lack of paid benefits, such as insurance, vacations,
  and Social Security
- Lack of support systems and collegiality
- Long hours
- A lot of selling
- No backup equipment or people

Is a Home-Based Business for You?

No matter what kind of business you're thinking about
starting, the first step is to take a hard look at your
personality, goals, experience, and skills. This kind of
information will not only help you determine if you're
suited to working at home, but also the kind of business at
which you might do best.

Mark each of the following statements with a true or false.
Be honest—there are no right answers, just different styles.
When answering, think about how you respond to both on-
the-job situations and experiences in your personal life.

Work Habits: True or False

1. When faced with several important tasks, I am
   able to set my own priorities._____
2. I have been trained to delegate work to others.

   _____
3. I don't like to sit in the office all day long. _____

4. I don't like making phone calls to people I don't know. _____
5. I prefer to work by myself. _____
6. It's important to me to be told that I'm doing a good job. _____
7. I am very detail-oriented. _____
8. I am good at judging how long it will take me to complete a task. _____

All right, we confess: Numbers 1 and 8 do have one right answer. But the other ones really don't. They're simply designed to help you see your preferences and strengths and weaknesses. A weakness in a certain area doesn't mean you have to give up your business plans. It just means that you need to be especially aware that this is an area that could cause some trouble for you later. Keep your weaknesses in mind as you're making your plans. See how your answers compare to the ones below.

1. Being able to set priorities is critical. Most home-based businesses are run by one person. In other words, regardless of what your business is, you're the boss, but you're also the support staff, salesperson, accountant, mailroom, marketing and advertising departments, and so on. Even if you do have people working for you, they're going to be looking to you to make the major decisions. You need to be able to determine what needs to be done— and then make sure that you follow through on it.

2. In most full-time jobs, the ability to delegate effectively is considered an attribute. It involves knowing what needs to be done, deciding who is best suited to doing it, keeping track of a variety of projects, and being aware of the various time constraints. All these are skills that can be helpful to you in your own business. But what if you don't have anyone to delegate to? If you're starting a one-person business, are you willing to do all the necessary work, no matter how tedious or time consuming?

3. Whether or not you end up spending most of your day in your home office will depend on the nature of your business. If you're an electrician, most of your work will be done at your client's; if you have a word processing business, you probably will spend a good part of your day at your computer. Keep your preference in mind as you research your business ideas and make your decisions about how to set up your office and structure your business days.

4. Most people don't *like* to make phone calls to people they don't know. The question here is really, "Are you *willing* to make phone calls to people you don't know?" Whatever your business is, a large part of your day is going to involve selling yourself or your product to other people. Especially at the beginning, you'll probably find that you're doing more sales than anything else.

5. Again, whether or not you spend most of your time by yourself will depend to a large degree on the nature of your business. If you go to people's places of business to sell a product, you'll rarely have any time alone, except maybe when you're doing the paperwork. On the other hand, if you're, say, a calligrapher, you probably will be doing most of your work by yourself. Many people are afraid of the idea of working at home because they think they won't have contact with other people. In reality, though, after your business gets off the ground, it's not unusual to find you have interaction with even more people than you used to—a range of clients or customers, suppliers, delivery people, and so on.

6. Most of us do need to be told we're doing a good job, at least once in a while. And we're used to hearing that (or hoping to hear it) from our bosses. If you're the only one in the office, who is going to tell you that? Your clients and customers. In fact, it's likely that you'll hear it more from them than you ever did from a boss. Bosses can become complacent. If you always do a good job, that's what they learn to expect from you. Your clients or customers will also expect you to do a good job. But since you won't generally deal with them on a daily basis, they're actually more likely to tell you how pleased they are.

7. Being detail-oriented is usually considered a good trait. And it is one that you'll need in your business. Forget to pay your suppliers or the phone bill, and you could be in trouble. Skip a step in preparing your budget, and your calculations could be all off. But there can be a negative side to being detail-oriented, if it prevents you from seeing the big picture. Make sure that you don't get so caught up in the small things that you forget or ignore the big ones.

8. It's essential that you be realistic about your abilities and that you be able to determine what's involved in any project. Particularly if yours is a one-person business, you'll need to be aware of what you can accomplish in any given period of time. You'll also need to be able to judge when it's time for you to get some help, whether in the form of a temporary secretary, a full-time bookkeeper, or a lawyer to help you prepare contracts.

Goals
If it still sounds like you might be suited to working from your home, the next question to ask yourself is *why* you want to start a home-based business. Here are some of the more common reasons. Your own personal reasons may or may not match these exactly, but they'll probably be pretty

similar. As you continue the process of deciding on a business and setting up your business and office, keep your reasons for starting your home-based business in mind.

- More free time (to spend with children, other people, pursue hobbies)
- Want to be your own boss
- The opportunity to do work you really like
- Bored with current job
- Recently been laid off or a strong possibility you will be
- You can't afford to start a business outside of your home
- The chance to make more money

What Kind of Business Should You Start?

The exact type of business you start will depend on your reasons for wanting to start a business, and what you're qualified to do. If all you know at this point is that you want or need to do something different than you've been doing, you might want to consider a professional career counselor to help guide you in the right direction. Career counseling typically starts with these four questions:

1. *What do you like to do?* List everything you like to do here, whether you see a direct connection to a job or not. Include parts of current or past jobs that you've liked, as well as hobbies and other things you like to do in your free time. You never know where the germ of an idea is going to come from. For example, you might not be able to make a living doing needlepoint, but maybe you could sell needlepoint supplies.

2. *What do you know how to do?* Again, list *all* your skills and training, whether it seems applicable at this point or not. Of course, you're not necessarily limited to a field you already know about or have training in, but it will indicate a natural starting point.

3. *If money was no factor, what would you do?* This question is sometimes phrased as "What would you *pay* to be able to do?" This is the place to dream a little. If your real passion is photography, maybe now's the time to try to make it into a business. Yes, eventually you'll need to be practical and consider whether or not you can really make a living from your business, but don't discard ideas simply out of habit.

4. *What would other people be willing to pay you to do?* Now's the time to come back to reality. Try combining what you know how to do with what you like to do. At this point, many people start off with jobs they've already held. That's fine, but take it a little further. Can you combine your skills and likes in different ways to come up with other professions? Your local library should have books outlining a variety of different careers—look through them for ideas if you're still stumped. Other ways of finding more information about various fields are listed in Chapter 2, under "Research."

Product and Service Companies

When you're choosing your business, you basically have two options. With a *product* company, you can sell items you make yourself (clothing, food products, crafts, and so on) or items that you first purchase from other people.

A *service* company is one in which you provide some sort of service, again either you own or someone else's. You can either sell your own typing, accounting, cleaning, organizing, or other skills, or be the focal point for the sale of other people's skills.

2 | *Start-up Steps*

Personality, goals, and skills, although factors in your success, certainly aren't the only things you must consider before embarking on a new business. If you already have a particular product or service in mind, see if you can answer the following group of questions. If you don't know all the answers or haven't focused on a particular business yet, keep these questions in mind as you gather your information. This chapter will explore ways to get information and other decisions you'll need to make before you open the doors of your business.

1. Is my product or service different from others already in the market?
2. Can I provide my service or product as well as or better than the competition?
3. Do I have the right kind of business experience and training?
4. Can I prepare a business plan for the next three years?
5. Am I willing and able to put in the long hours that might be necessary?
6. Am I prepared to stick with this even during the rough times?
7. Does my family fully understand everything involved in this idea and completely support it?

8. Do I have enough money to support me until my business starts to make a profit?
9. What will I do if it fails?

Research

The more information you have about your business before you start, the less likely it is that you'll run into unanticipated problems along the way. Specifically, you'll want to find out as much as possible about:

- Other companies in your industry
- If there are any similar companies in your locale
- How other people got started
- What kind of skills you'll need
- If a certain kind of training is generally required
- The market for your product or service
- Average prices
- Distribution methods
- Market trends
- How much money you'll need to cover start-up costs
- How long you should expect it to take before you make a profit
- How much money you can expect to make after you're established

The first place to look is the library. Try to find books about the industry you're interested in and individual companies in the industry. Find out if there are any trade magazines geared to people in the field. If there are, read back issues to get an idea of problems and important issues. See if any articles have run recently in newspapers or more general business magazines about your industry or particular companies in it.

While you're in the library, find out if there are any

industry associations for the field you're interested in. If there are, contact the association, tell them that you're thinking about entering the field, and ask them to send you any information they have available. This can include newsletters or magazines, a profile of their average member, salary and rate surveys, and a membership directory. Also ask if there's a local chapter of the association. If there is, attend some of the association meetings. You'll be able to meet other people in your field (quite possibly your competition) and find out more about the industry.

Speak to as many people as possible in the field you're interested in, particularly people who might have started with backgrounds similar to your own. Ask them what they did that they would recommend that you do, and, more importantly, what mistakes they made when they were setting up their businesses. Business owners of all types are generally full of "If only I had known then what I know now" stories—take advantage of that information!

You can also take classes to get more information about your field. Adult education institutions often offer one- or two-evening classes that provide an overview of an industry. For more in-depth information or training, contact local colleges. There are several associations and government offices that can provide more general business information (see chapter 13, Resources, at the back of this book).

Once you've read all the information available, it's time to move on to the next step.

Making the Transition

Assuming that you're still interested in your chosen field after all your research, your next decision is whether or not you're ready to start. Remember that *reading* about something can be very different from actually *doing* it.

If you're still working now, you have a couple of options for easing the transition into your new venture. One is to continue to work at your full-time job, while starting your new business on the side. This can give you security while you're starting, and also gives you an out. If you find that you really don't like the business you've chosen or can't quite get it off the ground, you can just discontinue it. If you do choose this option, be prepared for some very long days and nights. Also, make sure that your new venture doesn't present a direct conflict with your other employment.

Along the same lines, you might be able to cut your hours to part-time at your current job and start your new business on a part-time basis. Also consider taking a leave of absence to lay the groundwork for your business. If you're certain that you want to start the business, at least do all the preparation work before you actually quit your job. Get your financing, set up your office, start looking for clients or getting your mailings ready. Then when you do quit, you'll be ready to hit the ground running.

If you're not working now and are considering a career change, you might want to take a part-time job in your chosen field to see if you really like it. Depending on your industry, you might also be able to do an internship or volunteer work as an introduction.

Naming Your Business

Once you've decided you're definitely starting your business, you'll need to give it some sort of name. Look in the Yellow Pages to see how other companies in your industry are named. Many people simply choose to use their own names instead of a company name, particularly if it's clear that they're one person providing some sort of service. One advantage of not having a company name is that you won't need to set up special business banking accounts, which can be more costly than personal accounts.

Others chose to use their own name as part of their company names, such as "Bill Smith and Company" or

"Jones's Construction." If you've already established a reputation in your industry or your family name is well known in your area, this can be to your advantage. On the other hand, a name like "Bill Smith and Company" provides no clue as to what the company actually does.

If you're selling a product or want to give the impression of a larger company, you'll probably want to give your company a name. Play around with a variety of names. Try using descriptions, being cute, making up acronyms, including the use of your geographic area. You can even make up your own brand-new word if you want to (but be aware that potential customers won't know what it means if you use it solo). Write down all the ideas you're considering. Flip through your dictionary and thesaurus for more ideas.

Then start narrowing your ideas down. See if the names you've chosen convey the image that you want for your company. For example, if you plan on opening a corporate-gift buying business, you probably won't want a name that's too cute, while a dog grooming business can have as playful a name as you want. If you've included descriptive adjectives in your name, be sure you really want to focus on that aspect of your business. When "speedy" is part of your company's name, that's what customers will expect.

Once you've narrowed your choices down to about five, show them to other people and ask their opinions. Even if you already have a favorite, list a number of options. You'll get more honest opinions from people who are given a choice of several names than if you present them with just one.

You're almost ready to start now. The next two chapters will help you figure out if you already have enough money to start your business and what your options are if you need to get more.

3 | *The Bottom Line*

The last two chapters focused on intangibles—preferences, desires, goals. But, the fact is, most of us will need at least some money to be able to achieve those goals. "How much?" is the question. The answer can be found in your business plan.

For the moment, your business plan can be organized as informally as you want—it's the information that's important. If you do find that you need to raise capital, your business plan will be essential and should be formally organized and presented. First we'll look at the information you need to gather. Then, under the "Raising Capital" section of this chapter, you'll find an outline for organizing a formal proposal.

Your Initial Business Plan

You can find as many different ways to organize a business plan as you can find companies that have them. Basically, a business plan is a summary of all the relevant information about your business. For a small home-based business, you might never end up even showing your plan to anyone. Do one anyway. It's a good way to organize all the information you've gathered so far. It will also allow you to easily see any areas where you need more information or haven't figured out the details yet.

You'll find that you already have much of this information if you've done your up-front research thoroughly. Include the following in your plan:

- Company name
- Your proposed product or service
- Purpose and goals of your company
- Expected start-up date
- What qualifies you to run this business, including relevant training, skills, and expertise
- The training, skills, and expertise of anyone associated with the business (employees, partners)
- Your potential client or customer
- What makes you different from everyone else offering the same product or service
- **Your financial projections**

You were probably on a roll until you hit that last part: "your financial projections." Don't panic. Figuring out your real money situation can be a little tricky, but it's essential. You need to know if you already have the money to start and make a success of your business or if you'll have to find ways to get that money.

Financial Projections

In order to have an idea of how much money you'll need, first you have to figure out how much money you already have, including your present expenses, income, assets, and liabilities. Once you know your current financial situation, you can then make projections about what will happen after you start your business.

For some people, this process is much simpler than for others. A lot of the calculations can be estimated in your head without complicated computations. If you know you're always broke at the end of the week, it's a pretty safe bet that you'll have to at least match the salary you're currently making.

Don't be too hasty, though. Even if you choose to skip some of the following calculations, at least take a look at areas where you can save money and do make realistic projections about how much money you can earn. It's better to find out now that there are not enough hours in the week to charge the going rate for your service and still make enough money to live on than to realize it after you've quit your job, gotten a second mortgage on your house, and invested a year's worth of your time.

The following is one way you can calculate these numbers. You can use any other system you choose, but keep in mind that the goal is to be able to answer the following questions:

- What is your net worth?
- How much cash do you have or have access to?
- What are your current personal expenses?
- What are the anticipated start-up costs of your business?
- What do you expect your monthly business expenses to be?
- How long do you expect to work before you break even?
- How long do you expect to work before you start making a profit?
- How much of your own money are you willing to invest in your business?
- Do you have enough to cover the start-up costs and keep you going until you start making a profit?
- Where else can you get this money?

Current Income and Expenses
Before you can make any projections about the future, you need to know what your current money situation is. You can

make your calculations based either on the past twelve months or the past calendar year. If you've recently been laid off, you might want to make two estimations: one of your current nonworking situation and one of the situation as it was when you were employed. If you have a spouse or someone else with whom you share money, be sure to include that person's income and expenses as well.

1. Calculate your total current household income. Be sure to include your salary, spouse's salary, and income from any other sources, such as dividends, gifts, and interest.
2. Calculate your total current household expenses. Search your memory and records and include everything you spend money on here.
3. Divide your expenses into two categories: *Necessary* (taxes, mortgage or rent, utilities, insurances, food, clothing, car, household, loans, child care, etc.) and *discretionary* (vacations, entertainment, other luxuries). Since many people simply take a certain amount of money each week for daily expenses, it's not unusual if all you know is that you generally spend, say, a hundred dollars a week. Try to reconstruct an average week to see where that money really goes.
4. Subtract your expenses from your income. That's the money you now have in an average year to either save, invest, or play with.

Adjusted Personal Income and Expenses
Now that you know what you currently do with your money, you can estimate how that will change. First we'll figure out how much money you need to make, then we'll see if you really can make that amount.

1. Subtract the income from your job from the total current household income figure on your Current Income and Expenses Sheet. (Yes, if you're single that might well leave you with zero. Don't worry, we'll be adding something back in soon!)

2. Subtract from the total expenses on your Current Income and Expenses Sheet all discretionary expenses that you (and other household members) are *willing* to give up, at least for now. That might include vacations, expensive Saturday night dinners, daily lunches out, and so on. Be honest—if there's no way you're really going to give up your gym, exercise class, manicures, or weekly massages, then leave them in.

3. Subtract from the total expenses on your Current Income and Expenses Sheet any necessary expenses that will not be necessary if you're not working full-time. These will be different for everyone, but might include expenses such as transportation to and from work, dry cleaning, and child care (depending on your circumstances, this might be a partial saving).

4. Subtract your new expenses calculation (the numbers from steps 2 and 3) from your new income calculation (from step 1). It's very likely that will be a negative number (in other words, more expenses than income). Take off the negative sign and that number is how much money you will need to make to meet your *personal* expenses. If the number is positive (due, perhaps, to a spouse's income), your personal expenses, at least, are covered.

Projected Business Income and Expenses
You were probably able to do the last two sets of calculations with a minimum of guesswork. For the most part, you know how much money you make and how you spend it, even if there were a couple of surprises along the way. For your projected expenses and income, though, it might feel as if you're blindly pulling numbers from a hat.

The more accurate you can be with the next set of numbers you need to calculate, the better your chances of being adequately prepared to start and run your business. Do your homework. Talk to other people in your industry, check with industry associations, read trade magazines and books on your chosen field. We have divided the next task into seven easy steps.

1. Estimate the start-up costs for your business. Include anything you'll have to pay money for in order to be able to start your business. Be sure to include the following (for more information about what kinds of things are included in most of the categories below, see the chapter number in parentheses):

> Construction of or structural changes to your
> home office (Chapter 7)
> Equipment and furniture for your home office
> (Chapter 8)
> Office supplies (Chapter 8)
> Initial advertising, marketing, and public
> relations (Chapter 9)
> Professional consultation fees: accountants,
> lawyers, etc. (Chapter 6)
> Permits, licenses, registrations (Chapter 6)
> Raw materials or initial inventory (for product
> companies only)

2. Estimate what your regular business expenses will be. Calculate the monthly expense and multiply by twelve to get the yearly expense. Don't worry if you have to guess for some of these, but, again, do your research ahead of time. Don't forget about:

> Taxes (Chapter 4)
> Insurance (Chapter 4)
> Retirement plans (Chapter 4)
> Office supplies (Chapter 8)
> Advertising, marketing, and public relations
> (Chapter 9)

Salaries of any employees (Chapter 11)

Professional associations and trade magazines
   (Chapter 9)

Telephone costs (Chapter 8)

Additional cost of utilities attributed to home
   office (Chapter 4)

Travel and entertainment (Chapter 10)

Installment or credit card payments if planning
   to purchase equipment on credit (Chapter 4)

Raw materials and inventory, shipping and
   freight (for product companies)

3. Estimate what you can *reasonably* expect to make in
one month's time and multiply it by 12 for the first year's
income. Naturally, this also involves a fair amount of
guesswork, and there are some variables you just can't
account for, such as the overall economy, the invention of
new products that might make yours obsolete, and so on.
To get a rough estimate of what you can expect to make,
you'll first need to determine the pricing of your service
or product (see Chapter 4 for more information about
setting prices). Then:

For a service company: Multiply your hourly rate by the
number of hours you expect to work in a week (even if
you charge by the project, you should have an idea of
what it breaks down to for an hourly rate). Multiply that
figure by the number of weeks you anticipate working in
a year. This will be your total income. Do *not* include
hours you expect to spend doing unbillable tasks, such as
invoicing, marketing, and so on. Your hourly fee should
have a built-in margin to account for these unbillable
hours.

For a product company: Multiply your per-unit price by
the amount you expect to sell. As with a service company,
your per-unit price should include a margin to account
for unbillable hours.

4. Add your projected income from your company to your Adjusted Personal Income. This is your total projected income.

5. Add your projected expenses (start-up and yearly) to your adjusted personal expenses. This number is your total projected expenses.

6. Subtract your total projected expenses (from step 5) from your total projected income (from step 4). This is your total projected profit or loss for your first year of business.

7. The further out you try to project, the more guesswork is involved. For subsequent years, you can eliminate the one-time start-up costs, but factor in a cushion for emergencies, additional or updated equipment, and other unanticipated needs. If you've cut out all vacation time and luxuries, try to include those back in by the second or third year. Increase your income estimate if you think you will be working more hours, selling more of your product, or charging higher rates as time goes on.

Net Worth

There's one last calculation you need to make to really get a sense of your financial situation now and in the next few years. That's your net worth—how much you own versus how much you owe.

1. Add together the value of your assets—everything you *own*, including cash. Some examples of assets are the value of your home and your car (if you own them), investments, bank accounts, and other items of substantial monetary value (office equipment, jewelry, etc.).
2. Add the extent of your liabilities—everything you *owe*. Common expenses are money still owed on a mortgage or loan and credit card balances.

3. Subtract your total liabilities from your total
assets. If the number is positive, congratulations!
That means you actually own more than you owe,
and you might already have access to money you
need to start or keep your business going. Don't
be too upset if the number is negative—it just
means that, like many of us, you actually owe
more than you own. There are still ways for you
to get money if you need it.

Raising Capital

What do you do if you've figured out your potential
income and expenses and they add up to a loss? Your first
resource for money is yourself. Do you have savings to tide
you over until you can turn a profit? Are you willing to sell
some of your assets? Take a personal loan? Get a second
mortgage? Also take one last look at your projected personal
and business expenses—are you considering items as necessary that you really can do without for a while?

If you're still employed, there are steps you can take while
you're working to reduce your debt and otherwise prepare
yourself before you start your business. Try to pay off any
credit card balances so you don't have to worry about
monthly payments. If you have the money, start buying any
equipment and supplies you know you'll need now, so you
don't get hit with all the expenses at once.

If you own a home, establish a home equity line of credit.
Establishing the line of credit means that you have the
ability to borrow against the portion of your home that you
own. It does not mean that you actually have to take
advantage of this ability—unless you find you need to. You
might not be able to establish it once you've left your job, so
do it now. Even if you don't think you'll ever need the
money, at least it will be there if you do.

Whether you're currently employed or not, if you have

money in stocks or other risky investments, convert it into bank accounts or money market funds so you can have access to that money if you need it.

Where Can You Get Money?

There are a variety of ways for people with home-based businesses to get money, whether it's for start-up or for expansion. Before you approach anyone, whether it's your brother-in-law or your bank, make sure you've done all the necessary research and you know what you're talking about. The more informed and businesslike you appear, the more likely it is that someone will be willing to take a chance on you.

Be prepared for others to want to know the extent of your own risk in your business. If you're not willing to put any of your own money on the line, why would anyone else? This doesn't mean you have to put every penny you have into the business, but be reasonable.

The next few pages present an overview of ways to raise capital. After you've written your business plan and done your financial projections, you'll probably want to consult someone for more specific information about your particular options. Your local office of SCORE and some business associations can give you free advice (see "Resources"). *How to Raise Money in Less than 30 Days: A Learning Annex Book*, by Susan Wright, is a good source of additional information; you might also want to consult with an accountant or lawyer.

And remember: If it sounds too good to be true, it probably is. As the number of home-based businesses continues to increase, so does the number of people trying to take advantage of them. When you think of borrowing money, your first thought is probably a *bank* or other *commercial lender*. Feel free to try, but be aware that banks will not often lend money to new businesses. You do have some options, though, if you can't get a straight business loan on your own. First, if you've opened a home equity line of credit, you can use that. Second, you can consider a second mortgage on your home.

The Small Business Administration (SBA), offers guaranteed loan programs, in which a private lender, usually a bank, makes the loan, and the SBA guarantees up to 90 percent of it. The SBA will also make direct loans, although these are only available to applicants who are unable to obtain an SBA guaranteed loan. The direct loans are very limited and generally available only to certain types of borrowers, such as businesses in high unemployment areas or those owned by low-income or disabled individuals, or Vietnam or disabled veterans. (See chapter 13, Resources, for more information about the SBA.)

Although many people are wary of borrowing from *friends and relatives*, it's an option you should at least consider. If you do decide to ask them for a loan, expect to have to present your information the same way you would to someone who doesn't know you. Even if you are Aunt Betty's favorite niece, you're going to have to convince her that she's got a good chance of getting her money back.

Keep the transaction as professional as possible and verify it with a promissory note. That way, if you can't pay the loan back, at least the other person can take it as a capital loss. Also be aware that the IRS requires that the loan carry interest. If friends and relatives don't want to lend you the money straight out, they might be willing to invest in your company, giving you money in return for partial ownership.

Other options include *venture capitalists* (unlikely), taking a loan against your *life insurance* (risky), and running up your *credit cards* (expensive).

How Good a Risk Are You?
Anyone who is considering lending you money or investing in your business will obviously want to make sure the

money can be paid back or the investment will earn money. They will look at:

- Your overall character (Do you appear to be trustworthy, dependable, knowledgeable, committed to the venture, etc.?)
- Your past credit history
- Your background (Can you demonstrate sufficient expertise, experience, skills to make a profit from this business?)
- Whether or not you will actually have enough money to run the business soundly *after* you obtain their money (this calculation will consider whether you have sufficient funds for start-up and the initial operating phase and will take into account any possible losses during that period.)
- Whether or not you can demonstrate an ability to repay the loan

The Formal Business Plan

If you're trying to raise capital, your business plan has to be more formal than figures scratched on the back of an envelope. While the exact structure of the plan can vary, remember that this might be all a prospective investor/ lender has to base a decision on. Make sure the information is well researched, the organization logical, and the presentation professional. Be sure to include the following information:

- Cover letter
- Summary of contents of business plan
- A company mission statement (a brief statement of your company's purpose, objectives, and goals)
- A detailed description of the business you plan to start, including the product or service, structure, market, start-up costs, equipment, working capital, inventory

- Your experience, skills, and training
- The experience, skills, and training of any partners or employees
- Your marketing plans, including market analysis, competition, and projections
- A financial estimate of your resources and those of any associates (include any relevant financial statements)
- Your formal request for a *specific* amount of money
- A projection of your cash flow for the first three years, and specifically how you will use the income from your business to pay back the loan

4 | *Financial Decisions*

As we've seen, in order to prepare an effective business plan, you need to be able to calculate your financial estimates as accurately as possible. Often the hardest parts to estimate are those areas that the average person doesn't usually have to confront as an employee.

Unless you're an accountant, you probably never gave much thought to exactly how prices of products and services are determined. And while you may have had the opportunity to make some decisions about other major financial issues—like taxes, insurances, and retirement plans—most employees are only given limited options to begin with. All the choices can be a little overwhelming when you're first starting out, but persevere. Logical, well-informed decisions now can make a big difference later.

Pricing

Figuring out how much to charge for your product or service can be one of the trickiest parts of setting up your business. Charge too much and chances are no one will buy it. Charge too little, and you might be busy all day long—but broke. Whether you're selling a product or a service, there are three common strategies for setting prices.

1. *Cost plus markup:* For each unit of your product or each hour of your service, add your direct costs

28

(mileage, parts, labor, etc.) and your overhead
(office, supplies, utilities, and so on). To that
figure, add a markup for profit.
2. *Competitive pricing*: Set your price the same as
or lower than the market leader in your field and
area. You can add surcharges for such extras as
speed and guarantees.
3. *Market value pricing*: Charge as much as the
market will bear, in other words, as much more
than the competition as you can get away with.

As you can see, each of the above strategies requires that
you have some facts and figures before you determine your
price. The number-one thing you have to know is what your
competition is charging for the same product or service. You
won't necessarily charge exactly the same, but it serves as a
reasonable benchmark.

Secondly, you should know your anticipated costs, direct
and indirect. The third, and possibly most important,
factor: How much do you *need* to charge to make a living?
Here are some common questions and answers about setting
prices.

Should I charge the same as, higher, or lower than my competition?

Sorry, there's no right answer to this one. There are
reasons and advantages for doing it all three ways.
Charging the same as your competition is probably the
easiest—and safest—way to start. If you talk to five
people and find they all charge approximately the same
hourly rate or per-unit price, that price certainly makes
sense as a starting point.

However, in some industries, there really is no standard
price. Say you talk to five people, and get five different
hourly rates, ranging from $20 an hour to $50 an hour.
First, look at the experience of each of the five. Does the

one charging $50 an hour have a lot more years in the industry than the one charging $20? How about reputation? Are the ones who charge more better known in your industry or known for doing a particularly good job?

Don't forget about specialization and customer base. Maybe one works for multinational corporations and another one works for small businesses. Finally, look at how much work each person actually has. Is the $20-an-hour person turning them away at the door while the $50-an-hour person is always scrambling for new clients? Or maybe it's the other way around.

Ask the same kinds of questions if there's a range in product pricing. Does the higher-priced product have a reputation for being particularly well made? Has it been around longer so that it's just better known? Are some of the businesses targeting a higher income bracket than others? How about kinds and level of customer service? What is the volume of sales for the higher- and lower-priced items?

After you establish what the differences are, try to determine how your product or service fits in with the others. Be honest. You might be able to deceive yourself, but you probably won't be able to fool your customers—at least not more than once.

Should I charge an hourly rate or project rate for my service?

In part, this depends on what others in your industry do. Expect that you will not be the only person your customers contact when they need a project done. They'll be aware of what and how other people are charging. For example, if all the word processing businesses in your area charge an hourly rate, and you try to set a project rate, clients might be confused. In this situation, your price will seem higher—even if it works out to exactly the same final price—because you'll be talking about totals when others are talking about partial prices.

On the other hand, some clients don't want to have to think about how many hours you're working—they feel that's your business. All they care about is what they will have to hand over at the end of the project. If you're used to charging an hourly rate and are asked to provide a project rate, calculate the number of hours you think the project will take. Your regular hourly rate should already include a factor for unbillable hours, so you can simply multiply your anticipated hours by your usual rate.

An hourly rate is generally safer for you than a project rate, because you know you'll be paid for every bit of time you put into a project. On the other hand, a project rate can result in much larger payoffs. For example, you might generally charge $20 an hour for proofreading a business report and find that clients balk when you try higher numbers. But they might not have any problems when you say you'll charge $100 total to proofread the report, even though you only expect to spend two hours working on it.

How do I know if I'm charging the right price?

First, understand there is no "right" price for any product or service. There are, however, some factors you should consider after you've been in business for a while. The number-one question is: Are you making enough money to live on? If you're working as many hours as you can but still have no profit, you're probably not charging enough. Try raising prices gradually and see what the reaction is.

Also see how your product or service compares to others. Uniqueness, convenience, special services such as speed or unlimited follow-up, you or your product's reputation—these all might make it worthwhile to consumers to pay more. Remember, too, some people like to pay top dollar. It makes them feel like they're getting more, whether or not they really are. If your prices are too low, people may wonder why.

I realize I set my prices too low. How do I raise them without losing customers?

If you're raising your prices to bring them in line with what other people charge, your customers have probably been expecting this. Before you take the next project or order for the next sale, let them know that you have new rates that will go into effect on such-and-such date. Give people warning, though, so they have some time to adjust to the change.

Another option is to continue to bill current clients at the same rate, while charging new customers higher rates. You can do this indefinitely (there's no law that says you have to charge the same to X that you charge to Y); or you can phase in your new prices, maybe over the course of six months or a year.

If customers really balk at higher prices, consider continuing to charge them the current prices, but looking for new customers to replace them with. Particularly if you provide a service, it might be worth your while to hold onto them while you need their business. Once you find enough other clients who are willing to pay the higher price, you might find the lower-priced ones prevent you from taking higher-paid work. Or that it's just no longer worth your time to work at the lower prices.

Should I deal with clients who want to negotiate the price?

Absolutely. Even if you decide not to provide your product or service at what they finally offer, at least hear what they have to say. Particularly in the beginning, there can be several factors besides money that can make someone's business worthwhile. Does it help you penetrate a desired market? Will it give you additional exposure? Are they likely to refer you to other potential customers? Do they have the potential to become large-volume customers?

Taxes

Many new business owners are caught off guard when it comes time to pay taxes. We all know that we pay a portion of our earned money to the IRS. But it's not always as noticeable when it's taken directly out of your paycheck each week as it is when you have to make out a separate check to the IRS.

As a self-employed business owner, you will have to pay federal taxes, state taxes when applicable, and both the employer and employee portion of Social Security. (Depending on your business, you might also be responsible for state sales taxes and other state taxes.) Most home-based business owners pay estimated quarterly tax payments for federal and state taxes, including Social Security: April 15, June 15, September 15, and January 15. If you don't make these payments or are really off on your calculations, you can get stuck with substantial penalties for underpayment.

The total percent you're required to pay will vary depending on your income bracket. You can, however, expect to pay anywhere from 30 to 50 percent of your net income in taxes. One way to minimize the amount of money you owe is to take full advantage of all business deductions available to you.

Be aware that tax rules can change from year to year. Either consult your accountant or carefully read the IRS publications (see Chapter 13, Resources) before claiming any deductions. One example is the loss of any health-insurance deduction for self-employed people in 1992. Advocacy groups are currently fighting this, so it might still be turned around.

Here are some common deductions that home-based business owners can take. Again, be sure to confirm all your deductions before actually declaring them on your tax forms. Also, see the section "Records and Bookkeeping" in chapter 5 for tips on how to organize your tax information.

Home Office

One of the larger deductions for many home-based business owners, the state of the home office deduction is currently in somewhat a state of flux. The general rule for declaring a home office is that the office must be used exclusively and regularly for business purposes and also be the principal place of business.

The home office does not need to be a physically separate room to be taken as a deduction, but it must be used exclusively for business purposes. In other words, if the only function of your dining room is to serve as your home office, you can deduct it. If, however, you do occasionally serve meals there or do other household activities there, you cannot deduct the home office.

A Supreme Court ruling in January 1993 further limits the home office deduction. The case involved Dr. Nadar Soliman, a self-employed anesthesiologist. He performed anesthesiology in several hospitals and worked about ten to fifteen hours a week in his home office to do paperwork. No other office was available to him. The Supreme Court disallowed his home office deduction based on the fact that either the most important activities of the business must be carried out in the home office (Dr. Soliman's most important work was considered anesthesiology) or the home office owner has to spend the majority of working hours in the home office (Dr. Soliman did not). In other words, treating patients at the hospitals was his principal business, and the home office was therefore not considered his place of principal business.

Ultimately, the decision might have far-reaching effects, but it's been unclear just what those effects are as yet. In particular, the decision has worried many home-based business owners who spend the bulk of their day out of the office, yet still need their office for paperwork, sales calls, and other business activities. This can include any kind of business consultant, construction trades, traveling salespeople, performers, professional trainers, and so on. If you fall into any of those categories or are not sure about your home office deduction, be sure to consult with an accountant before you make your final decision.

As of 1991, IRS Form 8829 is required for people deducting a home office in addition to Schedule C (or C-EZ), "Profit and Loss From Business," and your regular Form 1040. To declare your home office, figure what percentage of your home is used for the home office. You can then deduct that percent of your mortgage or rent for the office.

Associated Deductions

In addition to the deduction for the home office, you can deduct other expenses that are related to the use of the home office. These include *direct* expenses and *indirect* expenses. Direct expenses are those that benefit only the business portion of your home, such as painting or repairs to that area. You can deduct one hundred percent of these expenses. Indirect expenses are those that are used for the upkeep and running of your entire home, such as overall repairs and maintenance, gas, electricity, and so on. You can generally take the same percent of those expenses as you take for your mortgage or rent (it varies sometimes, though, so read the tax form directions carefully).

Note that the combination of your home office deduction and indirect and direct expenses can't exceed the net income of your business. However, expenses that do exceed the net income can be carried forward to the following year. For example, your deductions attributable to your home office might be greater than your net income in your first year. The difference can be used in your second year of business when your net income will probably be greater.

Other Deductions
Some other expenses that you might be able to deduct include the following:

- Advertising
- Legal and professional services
- Office equipment (At present, you can deduct up to $10,000 on equipment, such as computers, copiers, and fax machines in a single year (you can also depreciate over the life of the asset)
- Office supplies
- Pension and profit sharing plans
- Taxes and licenses
- Travel, meals, and entertainment (80 percent of the total at present)
- Business credit card and bank account fees
- Postage and other mailing costs
- Dues for professional associations
- Publications related to your business (books, magazines, newspapers)
- Car or truck, if used for business purposes, including insurance, registration, gas, and repairs
- Business gifts
- Professional conventions and meetings
- Education for improving or maintaining required skills

Insurance

You're probably already aware that you should have health insurance, but there are a variety of other insurances—some more important than others—that home business owners should at least consider. The costs can add up, so don't forget to include them in any calculations for monthly expenses.

As you probably know, *health* insurance can run hundreds of dollars a month. Although the government is currently looking at alternatives, the number of Americans with no health insurance has risen drastically in the past few years. Not having health insurance can be a risky proposition. When money is tight, health insurance is often one of the first things to go. However, consider this: If money is so tight that you're considering foregoing insurance, what will you do if you do get sick; or need an operation; or ongoing high-priced medication?

Before you decide to give it up completely or buy an expensive individual plan, research your options. If your spouse is working, you may be eligible to join his or her plan. Since group insurance generally costs less than individual insurance, find out if you already belong to any groups that offer insurance. Most industry associations have insurance options as a benefit of membership (See chapter 13, Resources, for home-based business associations). In addition, check with your local chamber of commerce to see if there are any small business pools in your area that offer insurance.

Some insurance companies are now offering plans specifically for self-employed people. And some states are also taking steps to lower the cost of health insurance for self-employed and lower-income people.

Make sure you comparison shop. If you belong to more than one association or group, see what each of them offers. Just because it's a group rate doesn't mean it's a good rate. Also make sure you're not comparing apples to oranges: compare premium costs, deductibles, copayments, policy caps, and costs covered, including medicine.

You probably already have *homeowner's* or *apartment-*

dweller's insurance, but read your policy carefully to see if it covers your business needs. While a regular policy might cover personal liability if a guest is injured, it probably does not cover liability if a person is injured while in your home for business purposes. In addition, policies often exclude coverage of business property. See if you can add a rider to your present policy to cover these contingencies or consider getting separate policies to cover them. Your *auto* insurance also may or may not cover business use of the car. If not, add a rider to your personal policy.

You can get *business* insurance to cover general and product liability, the full replacement cost of equipment and furnishings, and compensation for a loss of earnings due to business interruption. Confirm that it is understood that the business is run in your home. You can also buy insurance specifically for *business equipment* or even just for your *computer* equipment. Be sure to find out if computer insurance simply covers the replacement value of the equipment or if it also insures against the loss of data, which can effectively be worth much more to you than the equipment.

Don't forget about yourself when you're considering insurance. If you are injured or you die, what will happen to your business? *Disability* insurance will cover you in the event that you're not able to work. Be sure to check how long you must be disabled before the policy kicks in, the policy's definition of "disabled," and for what period of time you can be paid.

Standard *life* insurance may or may not provide a spouse or other family members with enough money to keep your business going (if they want to and are able) in the event that something happens to you. Ask your insurance agent about *key person* insurance, which is actually a combination of insurances that will pay cash to the company, usually the policy beneficiary, when a key person dies or becomes disabled. Such a policy can also be structured to pay off company debt.

Depending on your business, you also might want to get *general liability, product liability, commercial liability,* or *malpractice* insurance. Talk to your lawyer to see if any such insurance is necessary for you. If you have other employees, also check with a lawyer to see if you are required to provide them with any insurance, such as *worker's compensation.*

Retirement Plans

It might be hard to think about retiring when you're first starting your new business, but eventually you'll need to start making provisions for it. If you don't have a lot in savings and you're not already covered by a retirement plan (maybe your spouse's), your financial security at retirement depends on your planning while you're working. In addition to the benefit of the money you put aside, you can also take advantage of substantial tax advantages now.

Retirement plans are available through banks and other financial institutions. Talk to their advisers to see which plan best suits your needs. Shop around a little, too. There can be significant differences in fees and options. Look for plans designed specifically for sole proprietorships and small companies. They generally require less paperwork and administration than those designed for larger companies.

Following are some questions you ask yourself before you set up a plan.

- How many more years do you expect to work before retiring?
- How much money would you like to have put aside by that time?

- Do you want to make annual contributions, regardless of profitability, each year?
- Do you want to contribute the same amount of money each year?
- Do you want a plan that requires annual administration?
- Is it important that there are provisions for loan or hardship withdrawals?

If you have employees now or think you might have some soon, also determine how long they must work before they're entitled to receive full benefits from the plan, and whether or not you want to include part-time employees in the plan.

The most common retirement plans include IRAs (Individual Retirement Accounts), SEPs (Simplified Employee Pensions), and Keoghs.

IRAs are available to anyone, self-employed or not, who earns less than a specified yearly salary (check with your accountant or financial institution to see if you qualify). There is a somewhat low limit to what you can contribute yearly ($2,000 at this writing). Your contributions are deductible, unless you or your spouse participates in an employee-sponsored retirement plan.

SEPs are retirement plans that are funded by employer contributions. One of the features that make SEPs attractive to small business owners is their simplicity. Generally easy to set up and administer, they don't require the complicated paperwork and government reporting that some other types of plans do. At present, the maximum deductible contribution is the lesser of $30,000 a year or up to 15 percent of the annual taxable compensation. One important advantage of a SEP is that you are not required to contribute the same amount each year, so you can make adjustments depending on your profits each year. A SEP is generally taxed as ordinary income when withdrawn at retirement.

Keoghs can only be set up by sole proprietors and partnerships (*not* the individual partner). They are more structured than a SEP and require filing annual information returns with the IRS. Taxation at withdrawal upon retirement may be more favorable than with SEPs. There are two kinds of Keoghs: profit sharing and money purchase plan.

With *profit sharing*, you are not obligated to contribute a set amount each year, a benefit if you expect variations in your business. The present limit on tax-deductible contributions is the lesser of $30,000 or up to 15 percent of annual taxable compensation.

A *money purchase* Keogh does require a fixed percent of compensation to be contributed each year. The maximum employer tax-deductible contribution is presently the lesser of $30,000 or 25 percent of annual taxable compensation.

Some banks and companies offer a third option, the *paired plan*, which combines features of the other two. A fixed minimum annual contribution is required each year, but you can also contribute a variable portion above that amount.

5 | *Money Matters*

By now you should have completed your own form of your business plan, including financial projections for your personal budget, business expenses, and income. If you haven't already relegated them to a back folder, you'll probably be tempted to do so soon. *Don't.*

While you certainly won't be looking at these papers on a daily basis, you will want to take a look at them every once in a while. The reasons will be fairly obvious, once you've made money matters an important priority in your routine.

Setting Income Goals

A good time to take a look at your business plan is when you do your weekly or monthly accounting. Use the plan as a yardstick to measure your progress: Are you meeting your original projections? If not, are you close to meeting them? Or at least coming closer each month?

After six months to a year, if you find that the reality of your business has no resemblance to your projections, it's time to reevaluate. Maybe you were overly optimistic with your sales projections. Or maybe you're selling the amount (or the hours) that you wanted, but not at the price you anticipated. It might be time to either readjust your price or to accept that you can't charge as much as you had hoped.

You might also have been off on the expenses end. Are you spending much more on marketing than you had expected? Take a look at the marketing results—do they justify the cost? Maybe your health insurance has skyrocketed or taxes have been increased yet again. You can't do much about factors like these except try to offset them by cutting back in other areas.

Of course, you might be meeting or even exceeding your original income goals. If you are, congratulations! But don't stop there. You should reevaluate in this case, too. Are you content at the level you're at, or is it time to set more challenging goals? Give some thought to whether or not you want to expand your product line, charge higher rates for your services, hire employees to do some of the administrative work you don't like or to sell your product or perform services. Maybe you can afford to update your office equipment or take that vacation you've been craving.

In order to make these comparisons, you have to be keeping accurate records of your expenses and income.

Records and Bookkeeping

Just the word "bookkeeping" can strike fear in the hearts of even the most practical business owners. Relax. It's not really that tough. If you can do simple addition and subtraction, you can do your own bookkeeping. Even if you can't, your calculator or computer software can do most of it for you—if you just take the time to input the information.

If, after reading this section, you still don't want to deal with bookkeeping, consult an accountant. If you do want to handle it yourself, there are several books on the market that explore business financial matters in detail, as well as college and adult education courses. Stationery and business supply stores sell a variety of record-keeping systems, and there are hundreds of software programs available. You might also want to consult an accountant for aid in the initial setup.

Bank Accounts

To prevent complete confusion, keep your personal and business money separate. The easiest way to do this is to open a separate checking account for your business. If you're doing business under your own name instead of a company name, you can simply open a second personal checking account rather than a business checking account. Business checking accounts are generally more expensive to maintain than personal checking accounts—they often include extra fees for every transaction, from checks written to deposits made to transfers from one account to another.

For people who are used to having taxes taken out of each paycheck (most of us), the amount of money you have available might be a little deceptive. Even if you're paying taxes quarterly, it might come as a surprise when you find that you have $4,000 in your business account on June 10, but $3,000 of it is due to the IRS on June 15. Consider setting up a separate savings account strictly for tax payments. Depending on your tax rate, you can transfer anywhere from 30 to 50 percent of each check you receive into that account.

Expenses

Many of your business expenses will be tax deductible (see chapter 4), but in order to declare them, you must be able to document them. Whenever possible, make your payments by check so you have your canceled checks as a record of your transactions. A separate business credit card also simplifies record-keeping, but interest payments can quickly add up. If you do use a business credit card, try to pay it off monthly.

Also keep all sales slips, paid bills and invoices, canceled checks, duplicate deposit slips, and any other documentation to support your transactions. If you do need to pay with cash, be especially sure to keep your receipts. If you forget to get a receipt, make a handwritten note of the item pur-chased, date, place, and amount as soon as possible. Don't forget to note the small items—calls from pay phones, bus and subway tokens, a business magazine or newspaper picked up in the street. Twenty-five cents here and fifty cents there can add up to a substantial amount of money in the course of a year.

For businesses without complicated transactions, the old shoebox method of saving documentation still works, although it's certainly not the most organized way to handle it. A relatively painless method of organizing your documentation is to put all of one month's records into a folder. At the end of the month, take some time to organize the month into separate folders of different types of expenses, such as supplies, transportation, travel, entertainment, and so on.

Be aware that you need to hold onto all your records until the statute of limitations for a particular tax return runs out, usually three years after the date the return is filed. In addition, keep copies of all of your tax returns. They're helpful for making year-to-year comparisons and for preparing the next year's tax returns.

Bookkeeping

Your system can be as simple or as detailed as you feel comfortable with, ranging from a checkbook recorder to a ledger to an inexpensive record book or sophisticated computer software. Most home-based businesses base their records on a simple calendar year (running from January 1 to December 31).

You'll need to decide if you want to use a *cash account-ing* method or *accrual accounting*. With cash accounting, you simply record when cash changes hands—income when the money actually comes in and expenses when the bills are paid. With accrual accounting, you report your income when it's earned (regardless of when you receive the payment) and expenses when they are incurred (regardless of when you pay).

Most small service companies and many small product companies choose the simpler cash accounting method. Accrual accounting is most often used by companies that keep inventory, in order to match income and expenses in the correct year and to be better able to see patterns. Once you select a method, you must continue to use the same one each year, so choose carefully.

The more detailed your records are through the year, the better you'll be able to track how your business is doing. A couple of minutes each week can also save major headaches at tax time.

Telephone Charges

For people who make a lot of long-distance phone calls, accounting codes are a relatively new service available from long-distance companies. They're useful if you want to charge phone expenses to a particular client or just want to track each long distance call. You create numeric codes of two, three, or four digits for each customer, which you enter after dialing the phone number. Your long-distance company then organizes your phone bills according to the codes. This service is generally free or low-cost, but some companies group it as part of a package, which may or may not include other features you want. If you frequently make calls from phones outside of your office, make sure you can use the codes from other telephones.

Cash Flow

Picture this: You're making major sales every day or working more hours than ever before providing your service. But when you look at your bank book, there's no money there. What happened? Two possibilities: Either your pricing is off (see chapter 4, Financial Decisions), or you need to revamp your collection system.

First check your billing system. Are you billing clients immediately? When you're busy with a lot of work, it's easy to put off your invoicing in favor of other "money-making" activities. It may be obvious, but it's worth saying: It doesn't matter how well you're doing if you don't get around to billing your clients! Make this a habit and a priority. The moment you make the sale or finish the work, prepare and mail the bill. No exceptions.

If it's reasonable in your industry, ask clients to pay half up front and half upon delivery. Particularly if you're selling a product, this can make a big difference. It gives you the cash in hand to order the product or materials you need to make it, instead of forcing you to lay out the money. Another option is to give customers an incentive to pay on time by granting a discount if the bill is paid within a certain time frame. For example, many companies print on their bills that there's a 2-percent discount if the account is paid within thirty days.

What about clients or customers who simply don't pay? As a rule of thumb, you should expect to be paid within three months, although this varies according to industry standards and any particulars you might have specified in a contract. If you have waited what you deem a reasonable amount of time without getting paid, start with a gentle reminder. Call your client or customer and ask—nicely—if your invoice has been received. If that doesn't prompt payment, a second invoice often does the trick.

If you still haven't been paid, call again and ask who you can speak with in the accounting department (assuming there is one) to check the status of your bill. In the meantime, if you're still doing work for that client, ask to be paid for the previous project or order before accepting the next one. If they can't pay for some reason, but you still want to work for them, ask if they can at least make a partial payment.

A drastic measure is to hold the current work or order "hostage" until they pay. You might get your money, but you'll almost always lose the client. If you still haven't been paid within a reasonable amount of time, you can hire a lawyer or collection agency to try to get the money. Calculate the cost ahead of time, though, or you might end up spending thousands of dollars to get hundreds of dollars back! A lawyer friend might be willing to make a phone call or send a letter for you as a favor—it's amazing what the simple word "lawyer" can do. Finally, if you can't get the money at all, check with your accountant. You might be able to at least write it off as a business loss on your taxes.

Although it always hurts your bottom line when people don't pay, you can keep it from becoming catastrophic by making an effort not to rely too heavily on any one client or customer. Many beginning business owners end up with one "bread-and-butter" client, someone they do most of their work for or sell most of their product to. Naturally, you don't want to turn down a client or customer who provides a large part of your business, but be aware that no matter how good your relationship, nothing is ever permanent. It's possible you could lose this client, either because of a change in management, shift in needs, bankruptcy, or other unanticipated change.

Take a minute right now to think about your customer or client base. Is there one person or business essentially keeping you in business? What would happen if you lost that business? If your heart's already starting to pound, make expanding your base a top priority. (See chapter 9 for more information about marketing and acquiring new clients.)

Barter

When you first start, and possibly for the first few years, money might be tight even when your business is doing well. One way to obtain goods and services you need is through barter. In its simplest form, barter means that you provide your product or service in exchange for someone else's product or service, instead of changing money. There are several ways you can achieve this situation.

The easiest and least formal method is to arrange barter with friends and business associates. It works something like this:

Kathy is a computer consultant with a new business. She has some clients but would like to do a brochure to hand out to potential clients. Tim is a writer who has just bought a new, sophisticated computer. He knows he can do a lot with it; he just doesn't know what or how yet.

Kathy, who has heard about Tim from one of her clients who does desktop publishing, calls Tim and proposes that she show him how to use his computer in exchange for his writing copy for her brochure. They agree in advance how many hours Kathy will consult for Tim and how many words Tim will write for Kathy (including whether or not she has the option to ask him to rewrite). Because they both know what they would generally charge for their services, they are able to negotiate a deal that is fair to both of them.

Barter works the same way for products as it does for services. If Tim sold office furniture and Kathy needed a new desk, they could arrange a similar deal. In addition, you can barter for goods or services that aren't necessarily business related, but which would be paid for from the profits of your business. You might be able to find a florist for your daughter's wedding, or someone to take care of your pet while you're away, or a chiropractor for weekly manipulations, or...anything. All kinds of business people engage in barter. It's often just a matter of asking.

Try not to get too carried away, though. First, even though it might seem as if you're getting something for free, you're not. You're paying for it with your time or product, which is worth money to you and to the other person involved. It's also worth money to the IRS, which expects you to pay income tax on the value of your goods or services bartered.

If you don't already know people you can trade with, consider a *commercial barter company* or a *barter exchange*. A barter exchange is made up of member companies who have surplus goods and services. This is similar to informal barter, in that Harry sells something to Brad, for which Harry receives trade credits. With those credits, Harry can then buy something from Neil, and so on. The barter exchange will typically charge a commission equal to a percent of the gross value of each deal.

A barter company usually does business with larger corporations. The barter company actually buys a company's goods and services, issuing trade credits as payment. The credits that you earn in exchange for your product or service can then be used to buy other items from the barter company. There is usually a monthly membership charge plus a charge equal to a percent of the value of the sale.

There are a couple of disadvantages to keep in mind when dealing with a barter company or exchange. First, it can take a while before you use any credits you have accumulated because there tends to be a limited selection. In addition, if you already have a lot of work, it can be frustrating to work or sell your product in exchange for credits that you might not be able to use immediately instead of cash. Remember: Although you can barter for a lot of things, you can't use your credits to pay for life's necessities, such as food, rent, and so on.

6 | *Legal Considerations*

Now that you've decided on what kind of business you want to start, you'll need to make some major decisions in terms of the way you structure your business. You'll also have to make sure you meet all legal requirements in your state, county, and city for starting your business. Unless your business is accounting or law, this part may seem tedious at best. But it *is* necessary—if you fail to comply with federal and state laws or make an error in setting up your business structure, you could end up with large fines, interruption of your business, or, in the worst case, have to abandon the business completely. So grit your teeth and read on.

Business Structures

Most home-based businesses start as sole proprietorships. Many never find a need to change that structure. There are, however, cases when it makes more sense to choose one of the other types of business structure. As you read through the descriptions of different ways to structure your business, consider the following:

- How much exposure to liability you are willing to risk
- Which structure will require the least amount of taxes (This depends to some degree on your

projected income and expenses and the maximum tax rates applicable to the various structures.)
- Your anticipated profits or losses
- Your probable need for financing
- The amount of money required to set up the various structures
- How the various structures can affect the sale of your business or succession to other family members

The specifics of each of the ways to structure your business can vary from state to state. The following descriptions are general. Consult a lawyer or tax adviser for the specifics in your state. In addition, the IRS offers various free publications on small businesses, partnerships, corporations, and S Corporations (see chapter 13, Resources).

Sole Proprietorships

This is the simplest form of business organization, and the classification that your business will fall under automatically if you're self-employed and the owner of an unincorporated business. With a sole proprietorship, the business has no existence apart from you. That means that its assets are yours—and you are also personally responsible for all of its liabilities. *All* of your assets—whether business or personal—are at risk with this kind of structure. The life of a sole proprietorship ends when you choose to end the business or when you die.

Because the business is not a separate legal entity, the profits and losses are filed on your personal federal income tax form and subject to regular personal income taxes. You are also required to file a tax form (Schedule C or C-EZ) for the business itself. In addition, you are required to pay your own Social Security, federal, and state taxes, usually by means of quarterly estimated taxes. In some areas, you might also be required to pay an unincorporated business tax.

The advantages of this structure are it's easy to establish, low in cost, and relatively free from government control and regulations. The disadvantages are you have unlimited liability and it may be harder to raise capital when necessary.

Partnerships

A partnership is comparable to a sole proprietorship in terms of taxes and liability, but involves two or more people who agree to share profits and losses, as they may share responsibilities. Like a sole proprietorship, a partnership is not a separate taxable entity. Its profits and losses pass through to the individual partners, who then file them on their own personal income tax forms. However, owners must still calculate the partnership's profit or loss and file an information return.

A partnership is generally required to establish a partnership agreement—sometimes called "Articles of Partnership"—which establishes each partner's share of income, gain, loss, and deductions, and may include the breakdown of business responsibilities of each partner.

Each partner is fully liable for *all* debts and liabilities of the partnership. In other words, if one partner does not pay his or her share, the other partner could be stuck with the full obligation. With a *limited partnership*, only the general partners who manage the company are completely liable for all legal obligations. The limited partners— investors who don't participate in day to day management— are liable only to the extent of their investment.

Advantages of a partnership are similar to those of a sole proprietorship, including little government regulation, few establishment expenses, and a lot of flexibility. In addition, you have the capital and expertise of two or more people, rather than just yourself. The major disadvantage is complete liability for all business obligations, especially if the other partner does not live up to his or her obligations.

Corporations

The major difference of a corporation from the above two structures is that a corporation is a legal and tax entity completely separate from its owners. That means that owners are not subject to unlimited liability.

As a separate entity, a federal income tax form must be filed for the corporation itself, in addition to the individual personal income tax forms filed by the owners.

The formation of a corporation is more complicated and expensive than the formation of other structures. It usually includes the investment of either money or property by the shareholders in exchange for capital stock in the corporation, filing of "Articles of Incorporation," payment of a state fee, approval from the secretary of state of your state, selection of a board of directors, and establishment of bylaws to govern operations.

There are actually two kinds of corporations, the *C Corporation* and the *S Corporation*. A C Corporation is taxed on its income, whether or not the income is distributed to its shareholders. If the company pays shareholders dividends, that money is then also taxable to the individuals. In other words, the earnings are subject to a double tax: first to the corporation and then to the individuals.

An S Corporation, on the other hand, is not a taxable entity. Its profits and losses pass through to the shareholders in proportion to their ownership interests and are then reported by the shareholders on their individual tax returns. S Corporations are not recognized by all states and are subject to more rigid government regulations than the other structures. Check with your lawyer to see if they are legal in your state and what the specifics involved are.

Advantages of either type of corporation include protection against liability (owners are liable only to the extent of their investment), and greater ease in transferring ownership and raising capital. Disadvantages are the amount of upfront and ongoing paperwork involved, more extensive government regulations, less flexibility, and more expenses involved in establishment.

Limited Liability Company
A relatively new kind of structure, the limited liability company features elements of both corporations and partnerships. The personal assets of the owners are protected, and there is no tax at the company level. As with a partnership, shareholders are taxed on business income at individual rates.

Owners must file an "Articles of Organization" with the state and establish a shareholder's or operating agreement that outlines the rules for managing the company. The rules regarding this kind of company are more flexible in terms of number and kinds of shareholders than the S Corporation. However, at present there are relatively few of this kind of company, which is legal in only about half of the states. Some financial advisers believe it will become increasingly popular as it is legalized in more states.

Other Legalities

Depending on the community and state where your business is located, it may be subject to a variety of legal requirements, including licenses, permits, and zoning regulations. Finding your way through the maze of regulations can be quite confusing, because there are different regulating agencies in each city, county, and state. Your best bet is to start with a lawyer, your local chamber of commerce, or your local office of SCORE (see chapter 13, Resources) to find out exactly who to ask about the various regulations.

Zoning Ordinances
Zoning ordinances are created at either the city or county level by various agencies. Look in your blue pages for the

agency that regulates zoning; common names are Zoning Administration, Building Inspector, and Planning Department. You might find that you don't need to do anything to work out of your home, or that all that is required is a simple license or permit. You also might find that a home office is completely prohibited.

Many of the zoning laws still on the books are hopelessly outdated, often prohibiting businesses of any kind in residential areas. Many communities simply choose to ignore zoning laws rather than deal with the hassle of changing them. If you're running a simple, one-person home office, with little or no customers, clients, employees, or outside traffic or disruption, it's unlikely that anyone will care even if you are in violation of the laws. Still, the laws do exist, and if you're found to be violating them, you could be subject to fines or even forced to stop your business.

If zoning is a problem and your business is visible, you can try to get a zoning variance, which basically just gives you permission to break the rules. If you're feeling really adventurous—and have the time and energy to spare from your business—you can even try to get the regulations in your area updated.

In addition to whether or not you can have a home office, zoning ordinances might regulate such things as outside signage, street parking, the number of employees allowed, traffic patterns, and sometimes even require or prohibit a separate business entrance.

Condominium, Cooperative, and Home Owners Associations

Many of these associations prohibit businesses of any kind even when they are permitted by area zoning laws. Again, many of these rules were established before home offices became so popular and are often, though not always, ignored. For the most part, they're only enforced when a business is considered "intrusive"—if there is a large volume of clients, customers, employees, or deliveries. For example, a psychologist or interior decorator who sees clients in the office might have a problem, whereas an artist who works at home alone, or an errand runner who mostly works outside of the home, would not.

Licenses, Permits, and Other Registrations

Depending on the nature of your business, federal, state, and municipal laws may require various licenses, permits, and other registrations. For example, hairdressers, locksmiths, electricians, plumbers, real estate brokers, and child-care providers are generally required to be licensed. State laws can also prohibit the manufacturing of certain items in your home and otherwise limit various aspects of your home business. Check with your lawyer, local chamber of commerce, local SCORE office, and industry associations to see if your business is affected.

Most states require that you register the name of your business if it is different from your own. In most cases, you'll receive a certificate that allows you to use your chosen business name and is also necessary for opening a business account under that name.

If you are employing other people, the IRS requires you to apply for an Employer Identification Number, used for income tax withholding, Social Security payments, and unemployment insurance. You can get this number from your local IRS office at no charge.

If you sell certain goods and services, you might need a sales tax resale number. This number enables you to purchase items for resale without paying a sales tax on them. You're then required to collect sales tax from your customers on all purchases.

You might also want to get a trademark to protect your company name or logo. You can sometimes register with state agencies, or you can do it at the federal level through the U.S. Patent and Trademark Office.

7 | *Choosing Your Office Space*

Many home offices end up in a particular part of the house by default—you set up the office wherever you have a spare room or just some extra space. Six months later, you have to move all your equipment, files, and supplies because you've either outgrown the space or you find you simply cannot work in the location you chose.

That scenario may not be catastrophic, but why go through the hassle of setting everything up and then having to move it all again? Since most of us don't have an empty spare room just waiting for us, finding the right space can definitely fall into the category of a "challenge." But it's worth the time it takes to do it the right way from the beginning.

What Are Your Options?

The first thing to do is look around your home and see what your options are. Remember that a home office doesn't always need to be a separate room. However, if you're planning to deduct the office as a business expense, it does have to be an area that is "used exclusively and regularly for business" and also be your "principal place of business." In other words, you can do all of your work on your kitchen table if you want to, but you can't deduct that area as a business office if the family also eats dinner there. (For more information about the home office deduction, see chapter 4).

All of the following are easy possibilities for home offices:

- Spare room
- Any room whose function isn't really necessary (a living room or dining room that is only used twice a year for formal entertaining, a guest room, a playroom that the children have outgrown)
- Portion of any room (including the kitchen, dining room, living room, bedroom, etc.)

With a little (or sometimes a lot!) of conversion work, these spaces also work as home offices:

- Basement
- Attic
- Garage
- Large closet, alcove, or storage space

Another option is building an office, either as an addition to your house or as a separate structure. If you're thinking about making large-scale renovations or additions, find out what these changes might do to the resale value and tax rate for your house. And try to keep the plans flexible—someday you (or the next owner) might decide to reconvert the space to some other use.

In addition to the obvious construction and labor costs, such as wiring for electricity, heating, air-conditioning units, and plumbing, don't forget to add in the less visible expenses. You're going to need paint or wallpaper for the walls, flooring or carpets, door knobs, light fixtures, bathroom supplies, and so on. The cost can add up quickly.

If you're already working at home or ready to start immediately, be realistic about your expectations. Construction almost always takes longer than anticipated. Where will you work in the meantime? Will the noise, dirt, and general disorder be merely irritating or completely disruptive?

What Are Your Needs?

For many of us—particularly apartment dwellers—finding the available space is the last step in choosing the office. We have one free room, or one area of empty space, so that becomes the office. If you're lucky enough to have a few possibilities, you can narrow your options be determining what you need—and want—to be able to do in your office. Here are some questions to consider:

Am I comfortable in this space?

Do you like the area you're considering or is it a part of the house you generally prefer not to go to? Physical factors can make a big difference. Are there windows that can be opened to allow fresh air and light to enter? Most people prefer to work in a space where there is at least some natural light.

Is the temperature comfortable? Does the space get adequate heating and air conditioning, or can it be wired to receive it? Is the area damp or humid? This is particularly important with basements and attics. Not only might you be uncomfortable, but it could harm sensitive equipment or supplies.

If you're thinking about partitioning off an area of a room that you use for other purposes, think about the amount of time that you might end up spending there. Between work and sleep time, do you really want to spend twenty hours a day in your bedroom?

Where is the space in relation to other parts of the house?

Do you want to feel "connected" to other activities in the house or would you prefer quiet seclusion? If you want to be able to hear when your baby cries, an upstairs room might be best; on the other hand, if you need absolute quiet to concentrate, a room next to the den where the kids watch TV every afternoon probably won't work.

Is there room for everything I need?

How large does the office have to be? It varies. For some people, a five-foot-by-five-foot space in a partitioned-off section of the bedroom is enough; for others a whole basement or converted garage might be the answer. First consider exactly what you want to do in the office:

1. Will I be the only person working in the office?
2. Will I meet clients in the office?
3. Will I keep inventory in the office?
4. How much storage, filing, and work space do I need?
5. Do I need a large area for work such as assembling products or packaging?
6. Do I have now or will I soon need large office equipment, such as a computer, a printer, a copy machine, or a fax machine?

If there is no space in your home large enough for everything you want to do in your work area, consider splitting up functions. For example, just because a caterer cooks in the kitchen doesn't mean he has to do his bookkeeping there. Or a pottery maker doesn't have to keep a year's worth of supplies in the same room in which she does the actual work.

Who else might be in the office?

If you expect to have other employees or clients in the office, you also have to think about a whole separate set of considerations. While a corner of your bedroom might be big enough to hold all your supplies, how will you feel if your client has to sit on your bed while you show your work? Or wade through piles of laundry to get to your basement office? Or see the dirty dishes in the sink as you go over ideas at the kitchen table?

If you expect other people to frequently be in the office, an area at least somewhat separated from private living areas is best. Consider, too, who the other people in the office might be. If you're going to hire your niece as your secretary, then you'll probably feel comfortable leaving her alone in the spare bedroom right next to your bedroom. But what if she quits? Would you want a stranger there when you're not home?

Other factors to consider are: Is there a place for other people to hang up their coats? Is there easy access to a bathroom? Is the kitchen easy to reach or do you have space in the office for a small refrigerator and coffee maker?

8 | *Setting Up Your Home Office*

Once you've determined the location of your office, the real fun starts. Remember all the utilitarian, dreary furniture at your full-time jobs? Well, you can forget it now! This is *your* office and you can outfit it any way you want.

Obviously, you need your office to be functional, but you'll also want it to be comfortable—someplace where you don't mind spending a good part of your life. Assume you're going to spend anywhere from one to twelve (or more) hours a day in your office—quite possibly more time than you spend in any other one room. What do you need to make this a place you really enjoy?

Office Furniture

Exactly what furniture you need will vary depending on the business and who, if anyone else, is also using your office. At minimum, most people need at least a desk, a chair, a place for files, and something to house supplies and/or equipment.

The Desk
It can be anything from the kitchen table to a folding table to your grandfather's rolltop desk, but you'll need someplace to do paperwork. This may well be the major piece of furniture in your office, so if you're buying new (or used),

shop around a bit until you find something that really expresses you and your new business. Do you want sleek and contemporary, massive, functional, ornate, old-fashioned?

If space is a factor, many modern desks come with shelving units and organizers built right in along the top. Another option is a folding desk unit. When closed, it looks like a storage unit; when opened, the desk pulls down, ready for work. Although you have to clean off the top of the desk before you can fold it up again, units come with built-in shelves and pockets for storing paperwork.

Folding up the desk at the end of the day can be a good way to "leave the office behind" when your office is in a room that you also use for other purposes. You can also build your own version of a folding desk into a corner, closet, or alcove.

Another space- and money-saving trick is to simply put a board across the top of two low filing cabinets set a couple of feet apart. This gives you a large work area plus plenty of storage space. To keep the desk steady, place the back of the filing cabinets and the board against the wall. If the board isn't sturdy, fasten it to the wall with screws.

The Chair

If you expect to be spending long hours at your desk or computer, a chair is the one item you can't afford to skimp on. The wrong chair can cause back pain and leg pain, and be a contributor to eye strain and carpal-tunnel syndrome if you're working at a computer.

Any chair you buy should have an adjustable height so you can set it up properly for your height and the height of the desk. If you're working at a computer, the chair should be set so your forearms are parallel to the floor as your type. A swivel chair with casters allows you to reach other nearby items easily. With armrests or without is mostly a matter of personal preference and what you intend to do when in the chair. Armrests are nice when you're doing mostly paperwork, but many people feel they're constricting when working at a computer or typewriter.

Be sure to sit in any chair before you buy it, but be aware that even a chair that *feels* comfortable might not have the proper support. Unfortunately, the only way to really find out is to sit in the chair while you're working and see how your back and legs feel later. When buying, make sure you can return the chair if necessary; then test it out as soon as possible.

The Files

Although the traditional choice is the standard two- or four-drawer vertical filing cabinet, you do have other options, especially if space if limited. (For a small office, lateral files are generally not a good idea. They take up a lot of floor space while creating unusable wall space above.)

Many desks come with built-in drawers suitable for filing. Small, plastic portable filing units can easily fit under most desks and be moved as necessary. Stationery and inexpensive furniture stores generally carry a variety of stackable plastic cubes, many specifically made for filing. Hanging vertical grid file holders can free up work space and take advantage of dead wall space.

If you don't have enough room in your office for all your paperwork, split your files into two categories: papers you have to keep, but don't need access to on a daily basis (old tax records, insurance papers, warranties, etc.); and papers you must have at hand. You can keep the ones you don't need everyday in a filing cabinet or cardboard file boxes in a closet or even in another room.

Storage Space

Like files, you don't need to keep all your supplies in your office, just the ones you'll need on a daily basis. The box of paper for the printer, extra envelopes and forms, toner for the copy machine can all be kept in another room or stacked in a closet. If you sell a product, you might want to keep samples in your office but the actual inventory elsewhere. If you make a craft, keep bulk supplies or little-used equipment out of the way in a closet, cabinet, or another room.

If you have the wall space, floor-to-ceiling bookcases are convenient for holding papers, computer supplies, stationery, and other supplies in addition to books. The kind you put together yourself are inexpensive and allow you to place the shelves at varying heights of your own choice.

Modular wall units are even more convenient because you can include some sections that have doors to hide items that you don't want to be visible. Individual wall shelves are another inexpensive choice that allow you to take advantage of otherwise unused wall space.

Other Furniture

Besides the basics, what you need is determined mostly by what else you will be doing in your office. If you expect an occasional client to drop by, one easy chair might be sufficient. If, on the other hand, you think you might be making group presentations, you'll need a table (separate from your desk) and a few more chairs. This can be a permanent setup or, if you expect instances like this to be rare, you might just want to move a table and chairs in from another part of your home whenever necessary.

Personal preferences also play a role. Think about offices you've worked in before. If you've found that you generally think better when you sit on a couch than you do at a desk, then by all means include one in your set up if you have the space. If not, can you choose a place for your office that's near enough to a sofa in the house so that you can easily move back and forth?

Maybe you feel most effective when all current projects are stacked on a nearby table. Make the table a priority. Do you like to work with music in the background? A small portable radio might do the trick—or you might want to move your stereo from the living room into your office.

Office Equipment

The controversy about what kind of office equipment to get rages on as new and better products are developed every day. Should you spring for the most up-to-date, top-of-the-line product? Stick with the old typewriter and rotary dial phone you used in college? Or try to hit somewhere in the middle? For many of us, the choice is moot—when funds are limited, you buy what you can afford.

Your office equipment can be as basic as a telephone and answering machine or as sophisticated as a computer, facsimile machine, and copy machine. How do you know what you need to buy and what you can pass on? Put any piece of equipment you're considering to these two tests:

1. Do you absolutely need this equipment to go into business?

Note that needing is different from wanting. You can't start a desktop publishing business without a computer. You *can* start your cleaning service business without a computer, even though you might want one to help with the billing and record-keeping.

2. Do you expect to use this equipment on a daily—or at least frequent—basis?

If your business is corporate consulting, you might find that most clients assume you have a fax machine and prefer to fax their information to you. A fax machine would then go onto your must-have list. But, say you're an architect who occasionally wants to send or receive faxes. As long as it's a once-in-a-while occurrence, you probably don't need the fax machine from the day you start your business.

You can always buy additional equipment as the need arises. But what do you do until you can afford to buy the equipment? Whenever possible, use other people's for free or in exchange for some service you can provide them.

For example, if you've left your last company on good terms, they may be willing to let you use their copy machine occasionally. If your next door neighbor has a laser printer, but never did learn how to sew, you might be able to use her printer in exchange for some hem work. Be creative!

When all else fails, hand the man across the counter in the copy shop the $10 to receive your fax. When you find that you spend more time in his company than in your wife's, it's probably time to spring for the machine. It's also time when your fantasies stop featuring the man across the street and focus instead on all the extra work you could accomplish if only you had a...

The Phone System

Many people use their regular home telephone to receive business phone calls, but if you're not the only person at home during the day, seriously consider getting a second, purely business phone line. Clients may not be too annoyed if they get a busy signal and have to call back again, but they will get upset (and you may lose the business) if they can't get through for more than an hour because teenager Tom is on the phone with his girlfriend or your wife is on a never-ending conference call hammering out the details of a contract.

For tax and record-keeping purposes, too, a second telephone number makes sense. While you can't deduct any portion of the cost of basic phone service on your primary home telephone, you can deduct the entire cost of a second business line. Long distance is another matter. Regardless of whether you use a personal or business phone, you can deduct your long-distance business expenses. The only difference is that with a personal telephone number, you have to go through all the calls and separate the personal long distance from the business; with a business line, the extra record-keeping is eliminated.

Many people who choose to advertise or otherwise promote their phone number get a second phone line so their home line is not listed. Even if you have two phone lines, you don't necessarily need two separate telephones. Multi-line phones are not nearly as expensive as they used to be, and some newer phones come with a "distinctive ringing" option, which allows different lines to sound different.

If you're buying a new telephone, it might be worth the extra money to get one with some or all of the following features:

Hold: This allows you to have conversations with other people or move around without the person on the other end hearing. It can be particularly helpful if there's a possibility of being interrupted by a barking dog, crying child, or other distinctly homelike noises.

Mute: This is similar to a hold button, except you can continue to hear what the person on the other end of the line is saying while preventing them from hearing anything on your end. It can be less disruptive than a hold button when trying to mask home noises.

Speaker: This keeps your hands free to do other things while the phone is ringing or you're on hold. But, face it, most people hate it when you talk to them on a speaker phone, so pick up when a person comes onto the other end.

Memory: This can be a tremendous time-saver if you frequently call the same numbers.

Automatic redial: This also saves a lot of time, and generally eases the level of frustration when you receive a busy signal.

Cordless telephone: This allows you to move about freely while continuing phone conversations. It also allows you to answer business calls from any other part of your home when you're not in your home office. (Provided, of course, that you remember to take it with you!)

What about other modern conveniences like call waiting and conference calling? The jury is still out on call waiting. Some business owners insist it's a sure mark of a home business and should be avoided. Others advocate it so that a client can always get through.

If you do decide to get call waiting, use common sense—and courtesy—when you hear the beep. Ask the person you're speaking with if you can put him or her on hold for a moment, then tell the second caller that you will get right back to him or her. Unless it's absolutely critical, don't accept the second call until you've completed the first—the first caller will *not* appreciate learning that their business is not as important to you as someone else's.

Conference-calling capacity depends completely on the nature of your business and whether or not you think you will ever need to use it. Many phones that have the above features also come with conference-calling features.

The Answering Machine

Regardless of what kind of business you have, an answering machine is a necessity. An unanswered phone sends an immediate cue to people at the other end that they are not dealing with a professional. It's also a good way to lose business. While a client will probably wait at least a day for you to return their call before calling the number-two person on their list, a no-answer is a pretty good way to guarantee they'll move right on to number two.

If you'd prefer not to let people know that you work at home, your outgoing message can be in a voice-mail format. Try a message like: "You've reached the voice mail of Susan

Jones (or company XYZ). I'm not in the office at the moment, but please leave a message and I'll return your call as soon as possible."

When buying a new answering machine, spend the extra money for one with remote access, so you can pick up your messages when you're out of the office. Try to pick up your messages every hour or so—an unreturned call can easily mean lost business opportunities.

A toll-saver feature on your machine allows you to set the machine to pick up, say, on the fourth ring for the first call you receive and then on the second ring for all following calls. When you call in to check your messages, you'll know that you don't have any if you hear the third ring, and won't have to waste the time and money to continue the call.

Other options include a traditional answering service and the call-answering services now available through most telephone companies.

The Computer

A computer can be a real time-saver when it comes to invoicing, bookkeeping, letter writing, and inventory tracking. If you have a good printer to go with it, you can also do your own stationery, promotional mailings, price lists, and so on. While most business owners love their computers, for many businesses, a computer is still not a necessity.

As computers become more popular, prices continue to fall and you can usually set up a basic serviceable system for less than $1,000. Or you can spend several thousand dollars for top-of-the-line equipment. If you do decide to buy a computer, whole books are dedicated to the topic of what kind to buy, including the questions of IBM models and IBM "compatibles" versus Macintoshes, whether you should buy one with the most advanced chip available or stick with the older models, how much memory you need, and so on.

When considering cost, be sure to factor in the expense of the computer accessories. Basics include a printer and software; other possibilities include a modem, integrated fax, and scanner.

Printer options are dot matrix, ink jet, and laser. A dot-matrix printer, the least expensive option, is sufficient for printing material for your own purposes. In industries where a strictly businesslike look is not critical, you can often get away with printing pricing lists, product information, invoices, purchase orders, and other material on a dot-matrix printer without jeopardizing any potential business. Many newer dot-matrix printers have options that include close simulations of laser-printerlike type.

The ink jet, a relatively new invention, prints in typefaces that fall in between the clarity of dot matrix and laser. The price of these printers also falls in between the two extremes, and they're becoming increasingly popular with small business owners who want a more professional look without the hefty price tag.

Laser printers, although the most expensive option, also have the most potential to help you make money. The crisp and professional looking print allows you to design and customize your own letterhead, personalized envelopes, press releases, product information sheets, and even brochures and catalogs. If you will be dealing with the corporate world, a laser printer—or at least access to one—is a necessity.

Software prices have also fallen in the past few years, but the more popular programs remain expensive, apparently geared to the pocketbook of the corporate world rather than the individual. There are, however, a surprising number of business and productivity programs—ranging from spread sheets and databases to word processors and graphics programs—available in the form of "freeware" and "shareware."

Both freeware and shareware are applications and utilities programs not generally commercially available, although in most cases, they are as useful as any program you would purchase. You can find them through on-line services and computer bulletin boards, or send for them through the mail. Freeware is free; shareware is usually free for a trial period. After that time period is over, users are asked to send a fee if they are going to use the program. Many of the program authors can be reached through on-line services and have support services available for registered users, the same as commercial programs.

The Fax Machine

More and more today, the question is "What is your fax number" rather than "Do you have a fax?" (Short for facsimile, "fax" is one of those multipurpose words that can be used to refer to the machine, the piece of paper that the transmitted material is printed on, and the act of sending information via the machine.)

You can buy a dedicated fax machine (one that only functions as a fax machine), or one that's integrated with another piece of equipment, such as a copier/fax, computer/fax, or printer/fax. One machine recently advertised as a "bundled" fax includes a plain paper fax, a backup printer, modem, optical scanner, and copier. Although the price for something like this is obviously higher than for a simple fax machine, it comes out much cheaper than buying each of the products individually. Integrated or bundled equipment is a tremendous space saver as well.

Office Supplies

Because most office supplies are generally inexpensive, many new business owners don't give them much thought when they're doing their planning. But if you need to buy them all at the same time, the prices can quickly add up.

You probably already have many of these items at home—move them into your office so you can find them quickly and easily. You can cut some of the cost by buying in bulk or purchasing through mail order or any of the office super-stores that are springing up all over the country. Do you have these items?

Pencils
Pencil sharpener
Pens
Stapler and staples
Staple remover
Tape
Paper clips
Rubber bands
Glue
Letter opener
Ruler
Scissors
Paper
    Note pads
    Plain paper
    Printer paper
    Letterhead
    Envelopes
    Business cards
    Stick-on notes
Files (hanging and manila)
Postage stamps
Typewriter or printer ribbons or cartridges
Copy machine toner
Calculator
Bulletin board and pushpins
Wall, desk, or blotter calendar and/or appointment book
Rolodex™

Putting It All Together

If you're like most people, you won't start out with everything you want in your office, maybe not even everything you need. But if you've done your homework and prepared well for your business, you should have years to add to, change, and fine-tune your choices.

One last word on what to include in your office—at least a couple of things you love to have near you. Everybody has their own personal items that can give them a lift or make them feel they "own" their space. For one person, it's a small photograph of a grandchild; for another it might be a bulletin board plastered with inspirational sayings or a favorite framed poster. While each person has their own individual favorite, some of the more common feel-good objects include special coffee mugs; executive stress-busters like Slinkys®, Silly Putty®, small punching bags, and plastic hammers; pictures of favorite people or places; good-luck pens; and diplomas and awards.

9 | *Marketing Your Business*

Wouldn't it be nice if you could just open your business and wait for the customers to line up outside? You can try that, of course, but you'll probably be in for a long wait. No matter how good your product or service, you have to let other people know about it. In its simplest form, that's exactly what marketing is: Letting people know how your product or service can fulfill *their* need.

Target Your Markets and Your Goals

Before you start any marketing effort, you have to know a few things about who you're trying to reach and your goals. You don't need to do a formal marketing plan, but at least write down the answers to the following six questions. Writing it all down on one piece of paper can show you pretty quickly if there are holes or inconsistencies in your plans. It can also show market niches and approaches you might not have been aware of.

1. What service or product does your company provide?

Be as specific as possible. Don't just write down that you sell food if you're selling homemade cakes, or that you're a photographer if you specialize in children's portraits. You might be able to find clues to an unusual marketing approach or your natural customer base in a well-defined description.

2. What makes your product or service different from all the others on the market?
Be honest. The answer might really be "nothing." That's all right, as long as you're aware of it. But give it some thought. Can the fact that yours is a small business work in your favor? Maybe you could stress the personal-care aspect. Or focus on being close by and convenient. Or stress that you are more aware of people's needs because you live in their neighborhood.

Are your products cheaper than other comparable ones? Do you perform your service faster or better than the competition? In the homemade cakes example above, one answer is the fact that they're homemade. If they're also all-natural or low-calorie or can be made to order, so much the better.

3. Who is your target market?
Be as specific as possible. The children's photographer would want to market to adults with children. But not just any parents—parents who have the money to have their children's portraits made. She might even have a more defined market. Maybe she's been told she has a unique talent for putting young children at ease. While she wouldn't have to eliminate older children, she could focus her marketing on the parents of preschool children.

4. What are your marketing goals?
To get more customers is the obvious answer, but there's probably more to it than just that. Maybe you want to attract better paying clients, or enough clients to work a forty-hour week, or repeat customers. Be as specific as possible here, but also realistic. The more defined your answer is, the easier it will be for you to see later if you've actually achieved your goals.

5. What, if anything, have your marketing efforts included so far?

If you've done something that's worked before, keep doing it! It's very possible that you're already marketing yourself and not even aware of it. Have you started telling your friends and family that you're in business or planning to go into business? That's marketing.

Now think about who you told. Were some people more interested than others? Did anyone tell you he or she would be happy to hand out your cards when you had them made? Be sure to take them up on it. How else have you let people know about your business? Have you gotten any business so far from these methods? What similar kinds of things can you do?

6. What is your marketing budget?

Marketing doesn't have to be expensive, but you'll probably end up spending at least some money on it. If you haven't budgeted for it, see if there are other places in your budget from which you can "borrow" some money. If you plan your marketing well, you should make enough money back from it to replace the "borrowed" money, have enough left over for more marketing, and hopefully some extra that you can take as profit!

Define Your Company's Image

Before you do anything else, figure out how you want to present both yourself and your company. Do you want people to know that you work out of your home? Would you like to be known as a small company that provides the personal touch? Or perhaps you'd rather give the impression of being part of a larger organization. Is friendliness going to be a factor? Or would you prefer cool professionalism? Is it important to show that you're on the cutting edge?

Or maybe your clients will feel comfortable with someone more conservative?

Defining your and your company's image is a combination of what makes you comfortable and what will make your customers feel comfortable. It's important to do this at the beginning so you can make sure that everything you do is consistent with your image. And the small things definitely count here. See if you convey the image you want in the following areas:

- The way you answer your telephone (A crisp, "Smith here" gives a very different impression from a friendly "Hi, this is Susan.")
- The message on your answering machine
- The clothes you wear
- Your stationery, including business cards, letterhead, envelopes, etc. (Consider the information you choose to put on it, the size of the various pieces of information, the typeface, the color, and logo, if you have one.)
- Your company name ("Beauty by Barbara" might well attract a different clientele than "Barbara's Hair Salon.")

Now that you know *what* you're trying to achieve, it's time to figure out *how* to achieve it. Assuming that you can't afford to take out a full page ad in the *Wall Street Journal* to announce the opening of your business, or hire a plane to skywrite your address during halftime of the Super Bowl, what are your other options?

Here are some low-cost marketing strategies that can yield big results. Try some, or all, of them and see which work well for you. Don't limit yourself—you can be doing several of these at the same time. Continue with the ones that work well, and drop or rethink the ones that don't yield results.

Network!

Yes, the old eighties cliché is alive and well in the nineties. Before you throw the book down in disgust, remember networking is really nothing more than simply telling everyone you know (and everyone you meet) about your business. You've probably been doing it for months— even if you didn't call it "networking" when you told your friends, family, drycleaner, hairdresser, electrician, and so on.

Now all you have to do is focus it a little more, if you haven't already. Have you talked to your ex-colleagues about your business? How about people who were your clients or customers at your last job? If you're in the same industry, they're a good source of potential clients. Don't forget other people you might know from your last job, such as suppliers, and even your old competition. You never know when someone who can't do a job or provide the service might just pass your name on.

Are there places where your clients are likely to be found? Go there! It could be anyplace from the supermarket on a busy Saturday morning to the golf course to an ultrachic restaurant. Be friendly. Try to strike up conversations. If the opportunity arises, mention your business, maybe leave your business card. Don't be too pushy. If someone is clearly not interested in your business, turn the topic to something else or move on to speak with others. These are not the kinds of places for aggressive sales tactics, but places where you just want to let other people know that you and your company exist.

If the people you're targeting tend to be in a particular industry, see if you can attend some of their association functions. If their meetings aren't generally open to guests, ask about joining as an associate member or at least getting on their mailing list so you can keep up with issues of interest to them.

If your potential clients are likely to frequent certain stores, see if you can post fliers in them or leave your business card or some brochures there. For example, if you're an accountant targeting small businesses, you might want to see if you can leave materials in business supply stores and photocopying shops. Try to get to know the people who work in these places, too. They're more likely to recommend you if they actually know who you are than if they merely have your card. Also consider offering a referral fee (or a percent of the value of the business referred to you) as an extra incentive.

Don't forget people who are in fields related to yours. That accountant might also want to ask his lawyer friend to refer any clients looking for an accountant. Also be sure to leave a generous supply of your business cards and any fliers or brochures with these people.

Stay in Touch

Networking is more than just making a connection: it includes constantly building your relationships. Whether you meet people in business or nonbusiness situations, be sure to follow up on the initial contact. You can easily do this with either a letter or a phone call. Again, this isn't the time for a hard sell; you just want people to remember you and have a good impression of you and your company.

Keep it simple: Remind people where you met them, tell them it was a pleasure, maybe include your brochure or any other information they've requested. It's important to keep relationships going, even when people haven't yet purchased your product or your service. One, you never know when they might need you. Two, you never know when they might be able to refer you to someone else.

Besides giving them information about your product or service, send them other information they might be interested in: industry press clippings, articles on related topics, comics or quotes that you think they'll appreciate. Call just to say "hello" every once in a while. But keep it short, and if the person seems busy or not interested, get off the line quickly. You don't want to be a pest, you simply want people to remember you. You might want to call people to tell them about an upcoming event or to see if they're going to attend some event you'll be attending. If you'll be in their area, see if they're available for lunch.

Look for Free Publicity

Believe it or not, publicity is one of the few things you really can get for free. Or at least without actually spending money—you'll definitely have to work for it, though. Keep in mind that magazines, newspapers, and television and radio news shows are in the business of providing information that is either entertaining or useful to *their* customers. They're not going to write about you or interview you or otherwise mention you unless you give them a reason to do so.

If you can get it, though, publicity often has more value than advertising. Being mentioned in an editorial capacity lends a certain credibility that advertising doesn't have. If you're mentioned in the press, ask to be sent a copy of the piece. Then make copies and include it as part of any promotional material you send out.

One of the easiest ways to get publicity for your company is to write *letters to the editor* of magazines and newspapers. Focus on local newspapers and magazines, and trade magazines of any industry you're trying to target. Agree or disagree with an article, describe a situation you've encountered that's similar to one recently written about, propose solutions to problems brought up. No matter what you write about, you must appear to have some sort of point besides pure self-promotion or the editors probably won't bother to print it.

If you or your company has done something interesting or unusual, you can mail out *press releases*. "Interesting" can include the opening of your business, hiring new employees, introducing a new product. People are always interested in stories of people who do something "good." If you've donated your products or services to any organization, let people know about it.

A press release should be straightforward and informational. Type the release double-spaced on your letterhead and be sure to include the date, a contact name, phone number, and address. Include a headline ("Local Company Feeds Homeless" or "Newtown's Flower Supplier Offers Special First-time Discounts"), a hook—what makes what you're writing about newsworthy—an explanation of the facts, and some quotes. Just be sure to target the right kinds of media and the right editor or your releases will end up in the trash. To find out who to send your releases to, check your local library for *Bacon's Publicity Checker* (for newspaper and magazine staff members), and *Bacon's Radio/TV Directory* (for radio and television reporters). Both can generally be found in your local library.

You can also make yourself available for interviews to newspaper, magazine, and television reporters. Keep an eye on current events to see if there's a big story that's related to your work. Has there been a rash of stories about the real estate market beginning to pick up? Then the news media might be interested in what you have to say if you're a real estate agent, a home inspector, or own a housing construction company. Taking it a little further afield, you might be able to show a connection if you're a gardener or interior decorator. Don't expect people to come to you, though. You have to let them know that you exist—and that you have something to say.

Make Yourself an Expert

If you know your business, there are probably other people interested in hearing what you have to say. "Experts" don't necessarily know any more than the average person: they just inform other people of what they know. It's more a matter of being visible than anything else. Here are some ways to get yourself in the public eye:

- Write articles for trade magazines or newspapers.
- Speak at meetings and seminars of industry associations (your own industry and any industries you're trying to target).
- Let people know you're available for interviews.
- Teach a class in your field. (Try companies specializing in adult education, evening classes at local high schools, your local "Y," community colleges, business organizations like the chamber of commerce, and industry associations.)

Try Mailings

Keep organized files for all your clients, both current and prospective. These can range from a simple handwritten list to a full computer database, depending on your equipment and the number of names required. Again, the idea here is to make sure people know and remember you.

The kind of mailings you do will depend to a large extent on your budget. They can range from short sales letters that you print on your home printer to professionally written and typeset newsletters. Don't forget about brochures, fliers, and catalogs.

In some cases, your mailing might be the only thing people have to determine their impression of your business. Make sure that anything you send out is neat, logically organized, professional looking, grammatically correct, and has no typos. If you're not sure, get someone to check it for you.

As with any other kind of marketing, mailings should tell the recipients how you can fulfill their needs. Consider including incentives to try your product or service, news of changes or improvements, special introductory offers, free trials, low- or no-cost initial consultations, and discounts to people who recommend you to other people.

Make it easy for people to get back to you. You might include a postcard for them to send back for more information or even an 800 number if you're targeting people outside of your immediate area. Don't consider mailings as an end in themselves; think of them as a way to begin or continue relationships. Before you send out any mailings, be prepared to:

- Be able to access information quickly.
- Respond promptly to all requests for information.
- Make follow-up calls after an initial contact.
- Continue to make check-in calls (even if you don't yet have their business).

It might be tempting to fax your material to prospective clients, but think twice before you do this. A law went into effect in 1992 prohibiting the transmission of *unsolicited* fax advertising. In order to fax material, you have to be able to demonstrate either a prior business relationship with the person or company you're faxing to or permission from the recipient to send the material.

Advertisements

Although advertising often costs much more than other forms of marketing, some advertising can be surprisingly low-cost. Consider putting classified or small display ads in trade magazines, local newspapers, association newsletters, and the local yellow pages. Monitor the response carefully to see if it really is worth your money to continue. Look at how many people respond, what percent of them actually become customers, and how the response rate compares to other, less expensive marketing activities.

You can dream as much as you want about the desired response, but be realistic when it comes to measuring the results. How many clients do you really have to attract to make the ad worthwhile? If the ad doesn't cost much, one new client in a three-month period might be all you need to justify the cost.

If you don't get what you consider a worthwhile response, first take a hard look at the advertisement itself. Maybe you're not really conveying what you want to. Ask other people for their honest impressions of your ads. Then consider where you've placed the advertisement. Just because it didn't draw a response when it was in your local newspaper doesn't mean that it wouldn't do well anywhere. Give it some time and then try placing it somewhere else.

General Marketing Hints

Regardless of what kind of marketing you do, be aware that it's an ongoing process. You can't just do it once and then sit back and wait. Your needs might change over time, so continue to evaluate your customer base and the results of your marketing.

Make sure you know who your customers really are. Don't be afraid to ask them what they like, don't like, changes or additions they would like to see made. Ask people who pass you over why they've done so. Then use that information. If their reasons make sense to you, try to eliminate the problem or change whatever needs to be changed. If one customer decides not to buy from you for a particular reason, it's very possible others have the same reason.

No matter how busy you are, make an effort to continue your marketing. Remember: It will help you keep your work flow more steady; and if your efforts don't pan out, a poor return on your marketing will be easier to accept when you're busy working than when you desperately need new customers.

10 | *The Daily Life of a Home-Based Business Person*

"The best thing I ever did" is the phrase most people use to describe how they feel about their move to a home-based business. But like anything else, it's not *all* sweetness and light. Many of the day-to-day problems encountered by the home-based business owner are really just a matter of adjusting to lifestyle changes.

While each individual will run into his or her own unique set of questions and problems, here are some of the most common ones—and ways to deal with them.

A Sense of Isolation

You're thrilled at the idea of not having to answer to anyone else, but the thought of sitting alone in your office day after day terrifies you. Fear of being lonely is probably the number-one problem people anticipate before they actually start their own business. In reality, most home business owners find their lives become even more filled with people than they were before. Once your business gets off the ground, you'll probably find yourself interacting with clients or customers, suppliers, and peers more than ever. But how do you get the ball in motion?

If you're feeling isolated, the first step is to identify exactly what it is you're missing. Is it simple human contact? Industry gossip? Someone to bounce ideas off of? Once you know what elements you want to add to your work life, you can set about finding them. Here are some tips for staying in touch with other people.

1. *Join—and become active in—professional associations.* They're a great way to meet people who are in the same field as you. You can stay on top of industry trends, discuss common problems, learn new techniques, and generally stay in touch with the people in your industry.

At the very least, attend regular membership meetings; many organizations also sponsor working breakfasts and lunches, and training seminars. If you have the time and interest, consider joining a Special Interest Group (SIG) or committee. Since they generally attract fewer people, all interested in one particular area, they can provide a real sense of community and be a good forum for getting to know the other people better.

2. *Stay in touch with colleagues from previous jobs.* Whether it's a short phone call once in a while, a lunch, or a whole evening out on the town, ex-peers can provide industry, company, and people news that helps you to continue to feel connected. And now that you're no longer intimately involved, the office gossip that used to drive you crazy can be pretty entertaining—and useful for your own business purposes.

3. *Schedule informal get-togethers with other home-based business owners.* Even if the people you get together with run other types of businesses, you'll find that you all encounter many of the same kinds of problems and frustrations. You might not be able to solve each other's problems, but it often helps just to be able to vent your own to people who can relate to what you're going through.

If you already know other home business owners, see if they're interested; if not, try putting up signs in local stores where other entrepreneurs tend to go. You might even end up with a whole new group of friends! However frequently you decide to get together, do actually schedule the gatherings, preferably for the same hour and day each time. If not, it's too easy for "not right now" to never end up happening.

4. *Give yourself permission to take "people" breaks.* If you're simply missing a "Hi, how are you?" kind of casual interaction with other people, schedule some activities out of your office. For example, instead of getting a messenger to bring something over to a client, take a few minutes and drop it off yourself; instead of purchasing supplies mail order, go to the store yourself.

These breaks don't necessarily have to be business-oriented. If you can afford the time, or are willing to make it up later, there's nothing wrong with having lunch with a friend, scheduling a daytime exercise class, or running some personal errands. Millions of people who work outside of their homes take advantage of their lunch hour to just get out of the office—you can too. Go shopping, take a walk, stop by the library, jog, get your hair cut, whatever. Leaving the office for a while will most likely give you renewed energy, making you more productive when you do return to work.

Other Family Members

Not only will you experience a time of transition when you first start working at home, but so will everyone else in the house. Whether you're returning to work or shifting from an out-of-the-home job to one inside the home, there will probably be some major changes for everyone to deal

with. You're not just changing your job, you will undoubtedly be changing major aspects of your lifestyle.

Realistic expectations and honest communication are the
best ways to prevent problems—and to deal with the ones
that have already begun.

Children

Change can be frightening to children, just as it is for
adults. The best way to allay their fears is to give them as
much information as they are old enough to understand.
Explain that you are starting your own business, what you
will be doing, and what kinds of changes they can expect.
Be honest but positive. Let them know how excited you are
about this opportunity and ask them for their help and
cooperation.

If you have young children, a home office might sound
like a great way to combine work with taking care of your
children. But many women (and more and more men) have
discovered it often doesn't work.

Young children need—and demand—a lot of attention.
Are you prepared to let your newborn baby cry while you
finish taking an order from a new customer? Or to tell your
most important client you'd love to discuss her project right
now, but you have to change a diaper instead? And do you
really think your two-year-old is going to play quietly for
five hours while you finish writing your report?

For most parents, some form of day-care—even if it's just
for a couple of days each week or a few hours each day—
eventually becomes a necessity. You might be thinking that
defeats one of your purposes for choosing to have a home
office, but it doesn't have to. If, for example, you have a
babysitter in your home, you can still leave your office for
lunch or breaks with your child. Or you might want to have
your child in a day-care center during the morning while

you do your phone and paper work, and then have him or her at home for the rest of the day.

Other parents form groups to alternate taking care of the children (but don't even think about trying to accomplish anything on the day you have five toddlers in your home!) If your business hours can be flexible, you might want to do a portion of your work after your spouse has come home or your child has gone to sleep.

For older children, establish ground rules clearly and firmly. Be sure to address the following:

1. *What are the limits of your office?* Is anyone else allowed in the office? If so, are there set times when they can use the space? If you do allow others into your office—say, to use the computer—make it clear that your business needs take precedence and you can reclaim the office when necessary.

2. *When is someone allowed to interrupt you?* Do you want your children to be able to come in and chat when the urge strikes (if you do, be warned—you'll probably change your mind on that one pretty quickly!)? Or only in the case of an emergency? And exactly how do you define an emergency?

3. *Will there be changes in household responsibilities?* For example, you might need to ask an older child to watch a younger child in the afternoons after school. If you haven't been working, you might have to redistribute household chores, such as washing dishes, laundry, cleaning, and so on. If you'll be asking children to do a lot more around the house, it's only natural that they'll feel some resentment. Try to explain as clearly as possible *why* these changes are necessary and express— often—how much you appreciate their help.

Spouse
Spouses, too, might have trouble adjusting to major household and lifestyle changes. If you've put a lot of money

on the line or given up the security of a full-time position it's only natural for a spouse to worry.

Even if money is not a concern, the decision to start a home-based business is often accompanied by other major reevaluations. It can be difficult to watch your wife go from homemaker to boss, or your suit-clad husband go from an executive with a staff of twenty to stuffing his own envelopes.

Even when the change isn't quite that drastic, starting your own business is often the fulfillment of a long-hoped-for dream or a second chance at a career you really love. Watching a person go through those kinds of changes can often be more frightening than experiencing them yourself. A spouse can only watch, hope for the best, and offer support.

You'll have to discuss the ground rules with a spouse the same way you do with your children. Set parameters of the office, when you can be interrupted, and what, if any, household responsibilities will be changing. A warning here: Many people have a hard time accepting the fact that a spouse who works at home is really *working* (see below for more on this). In other words, even though you might well be working more hours than ever, your spouse might just assume that since you're home all day, you can do all the housework, errands, and child care. There's one way to handle this. Smile sweetly and just say no.

Distractions

The telephone, television, stereo, refrigerator, bed, garden. Taking advantage of all of these when you want can be a large part of the joy of having a home-based business. They can also be your downfall. No matter how much work you have, it's just plain easier to take a break when you're in your own home with no one watching over you.

How can you tell when these things have gone from being a break or reward to being a form of procrastination? First, realize that you should and will take breaks of some form. It's only natural. Think about your last job. Visualize the chats at the copy machine, the times when there were no customers in the store, the birthday parties for coworkers, trips to the coffee machine, and so on. Most people cannot—and wouldn't even attempt—to work an eight-hour day without some kind of break.

Breaks only become a problem when they prevent you from finishing what you want—or need—to accomplish. If you really love to watch "Oprah" every day, go ahead. Just realize you might have to start earlier in the day, or work later, or do whatever else might be necessary to make up that time. Or, depending on the nature of your work, you might be able to work and watch the program at the same time—maybe you can plan to address envelopes, print letters, clean out file folders, back up your computer's hard drive, or anything else that doesn't require your full attention.

Working out of your home offers plenty of opportunity to be *reasonably* flexible. Longing to take advantage of that beautiful spring day? Bring your laptop computer out into the garden to work for a while. Exhausted from too many sixteen-hour days in a row? Take the afternoon off—but either monitor your answering machine or change its message to indicate you're out of the office for the rest of the day.

Probably the biggest distraction for home-based business owners are people who think that because you're home, you don't really work. Persuading them that you really do work can be time-consuming and frustrating, but give it time. Keep saying no to family members who want you to run their errands and neighbors who stop by to hang out for a while, and eventually they'll get the idea.

Friends who call to talk on the phone are another matter. Feel free to tell them that you're not available to talk during the day, but be fair to yourself. Did you enjoy short phone conversations with friends when you used to work full-time? Why stop now? If you can't spare the time or don't want to tie up your telephone, simply say you can't speak now and you'll call them back later. Do it enough times and they'll get the idea.

If you work at odd times, it can be a little harder to convince people that you're busy. Say you're taking inventory at 10:00 P.M. and the phone rings. If you really can't spare the time, let the machine pick it up. It's a pretty safe bet that it's not a business call at that hour. If you have a hard time not answering a ringing phone, turn the ringer and your answering machine down so you can't hear it.

Work Clothes

Another of the joys of working at home for many people is that they don't have to dress as formally as if they were going to an outside job. On the other hand, some people continue to put on a suit to walk from one side of the bedroom to the other.

In some cases, you don't really have a choice. If yours is the kind of business where clients might unexpectedly drop by or you spend a good part of the day out seeking customers, you'll want to dress as others in your field do. Of course, this varies depending on your type of work. An artist or writer might be expected to dress funky, a corporate consultant businesslike, a day-care supervisor casual, a cosmetologist functional.

But what if you expect to spend the day alone in your office? Should you still get dressed up? What you wear while you're working can dramatically affect your attitude about what you're doing. The rule of thumb is to dress as formally as necessary to feel as if you're working. For one person, that's a full suit and tie; for another it's a sweatsuit.

You'll probably find yourself dressing differently as you go through different periods. You might have a busy week in the office when you wear jeans every day, then wear suits the next week when you're calling on clients. You also might find that sometimes you want to dress more professionally—just to give yourself a lift.

Regardless of how you dress when you're alone, be sure that you're presenting the image you want whenever there's a chance you will run into potential clients, customers, or colleagues. If you live in a small town where you might do so at the supermarket, take the time to dress the part of the successful business person.

Feeling Overwhelmed

Part of the reason you wanted to work for yourself was to be in control of yourself and your work. But did you realize just what was involved in being in charge? Making sales calls, bookkeeping, filling orders, filing, writing letters—all those things *other* people used to do. Once you get the business going, you'll probably find that you're spending more time working than ever before. All of a sudden, not only are you not in control of your work, you're no longer in control of any part of your life.

First, stop worrying. It happens to just about everybody. Second, once you feel you're somewhat established, it's time to regain control. The next chapter deals specifically with time management, but for now, there are two things you can do to help put it all in perspective when things get to be too much.

Know when you need to stop—if only for a little while. Allow yourself to take breaks, have at least a portion of the day or night when you're not working, and at least one day of the week off. Make sure you get enough sleep and eat at least somewhat regular meals. If you can't allow yourself to do all that, then *make* yourself do it. If you're exhausted or get sick, you won't be able to continue to do anything. And the time you take off will make the time you are working that much more productive.

The second thing is to acknowledge when and if you need help. Does it seem like you're spending half your life stuffing envelopes or retyping letters, when you really need to be doing other things? If so, get someone else to do those things for you, at least on a temporary basis. If you don't have the money to hire someone, recruit family or friends. Make it worth their while, though, and remember they're doing you a favor. Have some pizza for your helpers, allow children to watch an extra hour of television, do your friend's bookkeeping in exchange for her doing your filing.

Another option, if money is tight, is to hire high school or college students to work for you. Often they can do the typing, packaging, mailing as well as an adult—for much less money. See the next chapter for tips on how to figure out when you should hire other people full-time.

11 | *The Importance of Time Management*

Freedom. No one to watch over you. No one to tell you when you have to finish a project. No one to say you haven't met your quota this month. No one to demand you work late tonight.

Except you.

And you'll probably be the toughest boss you ever had. After all, you've invested *your own* time, money, and energy in this venture. You want—need—it to succeed.

Because figuring out your daily routines, determining schedules, and setting goals all involve a lot of personal decisions, it may take a while before you get into a pattern that really works well. You'll probably find yourself making constant minor—and sometimes major—adjustments along the way as you discover what works best for you.

Establishing Routines

Regardless of the nature of your business, you'll need to set up some routines and systems for your work. Many people find themselves falling into certain patterns that they unconsciously continue. A better way is to make some decisions up-front about the way you want to run your business. If you find your original routines don't end up working, you can always change them, but at least you'll have your foundations.

If you quit your job because you're not a nine-to-five kind of person, then obviously it won't make sense to establish working hours from nine to five. Taking it a step further, if you want the flexibility to work whenever the urge strikes, you might find you don't want to set any specific working hours at all. If you can manage, that is.

Even when you work for yourself, you don't work in a vacuum. You'll have clients or customers, suppliers, other people you need to see or speak to during the day. The nature of your business will put some constraints on your working hours right from the start. Whether you're providing a product or a service, if you work with the corporate world in any way, you'll need to work at least part of the day when other people are available.

How much of an overlap you'll need depends on exactly what you're doing. A corporate trainer, for example, might have to make sales calls, do research, and perform the actual training during regular working hours, but have the option of doing the preparation at any time of the day. On the other hand, if you're selling any kind of product to businesses, most of your day will be spent making sales calls—from nine to five. Of course, you can still do the paperwork whenever you want.

Those who aren't targeting the business world have more flexibility. In fact, clients and customers may be thrilled if you have hours other than traditional work hours so they don't have to take off time from *their* jobs to see or speak with you. Examples include interior decorators, calligraphers, doctors, accountants, dressmakers—anyone whose clients tend to be individuals rather than businesses.

When planning your day, you can establish your routines as rigidly or flexibly as you want. Some people like to know that from nine to ten, they'll do all their paperwork; others might plan to do all their paperwork first thing in the day, but leave what hour they start a variable. For other people, scheduling by the day works better than scheduling by the hour, planning paperwork for Mondays, sales calls for Tuesdays, and so on.

Regardless of which method you choose, even people with the strictest routines will need to vary from them at times. You certainly can't tell a customer that you can't send their rush order out for them today because today's Tuesday and you do your mailings on Thursdays. Or wait until your regular phone hour at three o'clock to return a phone call from an important client received at ten o'clock.

Here are some decisions to think about when planning your work week:

1. How many hours a day you will work
2. If you will work predetermined hours each day or leave the exact times flexible
3. How many days of the week you will work
4. Which days you plan to work
5. Whether you want to schedule breaks and lunch hours or take them as needed
6. Whether you want to schedule activities for specific times of the day or days of the week or do them as necessary

It's likely you won't stick to what you originally determine, but at least you'll have some guidelines to start with. After a couple of months, once you get into the rhythm of your business, you can reevaluate and make more realistic determinations. Remember, too, there are natural rhythms in every business, whether they're weekly, monthly, or yearly. Most personal product sales, for example, fall off in July and are extra heavy in December. Some industries are busier at the beginning of the month than at the end; others might be stronger on Wednesdays than on Mondays. It may take a while to see these trends, particularly if you're new to your industry.

Once you have an idea of how much and when you want

to work, you can move on to the specifics. There are two ways to approach working out of your home. One way is to keep your work life and personal life completely separate, with well-defined time allocations for each. The other is to allow the two to merge—working when necessary, taking care of personal chores when necessary.

Although many business experts advocate keeping the two areas of your life completely separate, it's easier to say than to do. Even when people work outside of their homes, personal phone calls, errands, and the like tend to interfere with work hours to some degree. When you're actually in your home, it's much easier for the two to merge without even being aware of it.

Is it really a problem if the two aren't totally separate? Only if it prevents you from achieving what you want to do in a given business day. And there are times when mingling the two is unquestionably the most effective way to use your time. If, say, your dry cleaner is next door to the post office, it certainly makes sense to plan to stop in at both places on the same trip out of the house. Or, even though you might not usually consider doing housework a "break," you might want to do the dishes or vacuum or something along those lines when you just need to get up and move around a little.

Daily Planning

The "to-do" list—in any of its various forms—is undoubtedly any business owner's most necessary tool. These days options range from writing down things to do on a plain piece of paper to sophisticated computer programs, from the old calendar standby to elaborate executive organizers.

Which method you choose is a matter of personal preference, but regardless of the method, there are some general guidelines to keep in mind when planning your day.

The first is to be aware of your energy levels during the

day. Everyone has times when they feel particularly effective and other times when they're just not going to accomplish all that much. Monitor yourself for a week and see when your high and low periods occur. Then keep them in mind as you plan your days, scheduling your most difficult tasks for the time of day when you have the most energy.

For instance, if you're not a morning person, don't plan to come in and dive right into your work. Instead, allow yourself to ease into the day by reading your mail, cleaning up paperwork, making routine phone calls. On the other hand, if morning is your peak time, use it to make sales calls, work on demanding projects, and perform other activities that require your full attention.

At the end of each day, clarify your goals for the next day. Write down everything that you know you want to accomplish, including phone calls, appointments, errands, projects, and so on. If you tend to mix your business and personal lives, be sure to include personal items on the same list. Then divide the list into three categories: "must do," "should do," and "would like to do," given the time.

No matter how many things you end up with on your list, you'll sleep better at night at least knowing what the next day will bring. Everything seems more manageable when you've actually written it down than when you just let it all roll around undefined in your head.

Keep a separate list nearby of things you know you need to do in the near future, but that aren't yet a priority. That will help ensure you won't forget them when the time comes, keep you aware of what's coming up, and give you something to do if you happen to find yourself with some free time. Be sure to consult this master list as you make out your daily lists.

Check your daily list first thing in the morning and make sure that nothing has happened to change your priorities. As you finish each item, check it off. Continue to add to the list during the day as you think of other things you have to do. Whatever's left at the end of the day can be immediately transferred to the next day's list. If you find you keep transferring the same things, take a moment to reevaluate whether or not you really need to do them. You might find that you can eliminate them altogether—or that they've now become a priority.

In the same vein, make a more general "to-do" list on Friday (or whatever day you choose to mark the end of your week). It's a good way to wind down at the end of the week, and allows you to jump right in on Monday. As you're planning your week, try to gang activities when it makes sense to do so. If you know you're going to see a client on Tuesday, schedule lunch with your friend who lives in the same neighborhood for the same day. Or plan all your sales calls in one part of the city around each other. On the other hand, if you know you like to spend at least part of each day out of the office, make an effort to spread out activities that will take you outside.

Don't forget to block out your days off and vacations. Days off don't have to be Saturday and Sunday; it might make more sense for you to take, say, a Wednesday, instead. Either way, treat your days off the way you would any other scheduled task—don't violate it unless absolutely necessary. In the beginning, vacations will be harder to plan. You might not know your work load or even if it's financially possible for you to take time off. If you can't plan a long vacation, at least try to take an occasional long weekend until you get more settled.

Setting Goals

In addition to helping plan your everyday activities, daily and weekly lists will also help you see how much you really do accomplish in a given time period. Monitor your daily and weekly lists on a regular basis to see if you're being realistic and achieving your goals. For instance, take a look at what you've done in the past week. Did you complete everything you planned to do? If no, why not? Did something unexpected come up? Does something unexpected *always* come up?

Don't forget to also look at the big picture once in a while. Where do you want to be next year this time? Where would you like to be in five years? Are you meeting the goals you originally set for yourself? Why or why not? Is there anything you can change to better meet them?

Keep in mind your original reasons for wanting to start your own business. Along the way, you might find that you need to make some trade-offs. If you wanted to make 30 percent more money than you did working full-time, yet also have more time to spend with your children, one or the other of those goals might have to be readjusted, at least temporarily.

When you're setting your goals and making your lists, remember you're not super(wo)man. If you never come anywhere near accomplishing everything you want to, you're probably expecting too much from yourself. Either cut down on what you're trying to accomplish or make arrangements to get outside help.

Handling Overload

Best case scenario: Your business has really taken off, and there's so much work you just can't keep up with it all. Unrealistic? Not at all. If your business really is viable, you might even find yourself in the enviable position of sometimes having to turn down work. How do you handle those times when you really don't think you'll ever finish everything?

First, don't be *too* much of a perfectionist. It's your investment, your name, your product or service—of course, you want everything you do to be perfect. And if you weren't doing it well in the first place, you wouldn't have so much work now. But you do have to be aware of when "not perfect" is "good enough."

You might have wanted to have your proposal professionally typeset and bound, but you're running out of time. Will you lose the business if you print it on your laser printer and put it in a clear folder instead? Or will your customer be upset if you use mauve ribbons instead of dusty rose ones in the gift basket? Will anyone besides you even know the difference? In many cases, the answer is no.

If you're scheduling and monitoring yourself and still not getting as much done as you want, take a look at the details.

1. Are your phone numbers all together in one easily accessible place or do you have to search each time you want to call someone?
2. Are your files organized logically or are you constantly forgetting your own system?
3. Are all your supplies accessible and organized in a way you can find them?
4. Do you make a point of calling people when they are likely to be available? Or do you end up being constantly interrupted as people return your phone calls?
5. Do you take advantage of your time on hold by doing easily interruptable tasks such as printing, filing, stamping envelopes, sorting your mail? How about the time you spend waiting to see clients?
6. Be honest: Are you truly overloaded with work or are you really just procrastinating?

Procrastination can be insidious. We get so good at it, we often don't even realize we're doing it. Face it, sometimes there are things you'd just rather not do. So how do you get yourself to do them? Trick yourself. Promise yourself a reward when you finish it, whether it's an hour off, a new computer screen saver, or a personal treat like a massage.

Use the old standby of breaking it down into smaller tasks (it really does work!). It's much easier to schedule and complete several small projects than one large, overwhelming one. Also accept that you don't have to do it perfectly— at least not at the beginning. Just get something done; you can always go back and do the fine-tuning later.

If you're constantly having problems getting your work started or finished, reevaluate the kind of work that you've chosen. It might be hard to admit, but maybe you really don't like the work itself. Or maybe working at home really isn't for you. On the other hand, you might just be in a slump and need something new to break up your routine.

If you're doing all the above and still can't finish everything, you have two options. You can be more discriminating and stop accepting every project or order you get. As difficult as it might be to turn down work, examine every opportunity that comes your way. Is there a real reason to take it? Have you gotten to the point where you can say no to difficult customers, or those who don't pay as well, or those who propose things that you simply don't want to do?

The other option is to get some help with tasks that you either don't like, don't do as well as others, or are too time-consuming. You're probably working now without any support staff—no secretary, mail room, public relations people, or staff to whom you can delegate work. You're very possibly even doing your own accounting and contracts. Again, you have two options: either hire someone (part- or full-time) to come into your office to work or farm out the work. For example, you can hire someone to do word processing in your office every day or you can hire someone to do it from their home or place of business.

If you do have people come in and work, be aware that you'll lose some of your privacy and flexibility. Do extensive interviews and reference checking—after all, these people are going to be in your *home*. Also be sure to check all state and federal regulations concerning taxes, liability, and other legal issues.

Another way to keep your day more manageable is to take advantage of some of the same things you would do if you were working full-time in an outside office. It's not unusual for office employees to ask a secretary to hold all calls, or put their phone on voice-mail, or just close the office door so they won't be interrupted. You can do the same kinds of things. If you find that you're constantly interrupted by the telephone, turn down the bell and put your answering machine on. Set a time of the day when you'll check messages and return phone calls.

High-level executives sometimes take the day off to work at home when they're overloaded at the office. You can simulate that experience either by not answering phone calls for the day, or deciding to do your work outside of your office for the day, whether in your living room, a friend's office, the library, even a coffee shop.

Giving yourself some sort of break at times like this is critical. If you have to work Saturday, at least let yourself go out for dinner Saturday night; consciously make the decision to take an evening off and watch television or go to bed early. If you're exhausted and just plain burnt-out, you'll find that even when you are working, you're not achieving too much. Time "wasted" with breaks will actually make you that much more effective.

Dealing With Slow Business Times

Managing your time can actually be more difficult when you're not busy than when you are busy. When you're overloaded with work, somehow you always manage to get it all done. But what do you do when you find yourself sitting in your office day after day with nothing to do?

It's natural to be somewhat afraid at times like this. You might be wondering if anyone will ever call again or send in another order. You're likely calculating how much money you have and how long it will tide you over. If you have other employees, you're probably worrying about paying them—and keeping them busy during the time they're paid to be in the office.

Before you panic and consider closing up shop, take an objective look at the facts. Ask yourself these questions:

1. How is business this quarter compared to the last quarter?
2. How is business so far this year?
3. Are you meeting the goals you originally set for yourself?
4. If you've been in business for more than a year, how is this year compared to last year?
5. Has your business gone through a slow period before?
6. If so, were you able to identify a reason?
7. Is it likely that this slow period is due to the same reason?
8. Is there any action you can take to combat that reason?
9. Is the competition experiencing the same kind of slump?
10. Has the market changed?

You might find that this time of the year is just a slow period for your industry. Talk to other people who are in the same kind of business and see what they're experiencing. If it's just part of the nature of your business to be slow in, say,

September, try to relax and take advantage of the time to do all the things you never have time to do.

Whether it's a slump that everyone is experiencing or just something you're going through, try to make use of the downtime, particularly to increase your marketing efforts. (See chapter 9 for more information about marketing.) This is also the time to pull out your list of things to do "someday," whether it's updating your mailing list, cleaning out your computer files, targeting new clients, catching up on your trade magazine reading, or any other large, noncritical projects.

Use the time to take current or prospective clients out to lunch (or breakfast if money is tight), take a day off, talk to people in your field, research related businesses that you might be able to incorporate into your own. And make a point of going out socially and doing other things you find enjoyable to keep yourself in a good frame of mind. While it might be tempting to wallow in feeling bad, it certainly won't help the situation.

12 | *Moving Out*

It might be hard to imagine now, but the day might come when you start wondering if it's time to move out of your home office. The most obvious reason for moving out is lack of space, but other factors can also play a part. Some people simply find they don't like to work out of the home. Others love it for a while before they start missing some of the aspects of office or store life.

How do you know if it's time to move out? First ask yourself if you really want to move out of your home office or if you've just outgrown it. If you still want to work from your home, but don't have the room, make sure you've looked into the following options:

- Are there other rooms you can take over for your business in addition to the one(s) you have now?
- Do you have the property and money to build an addition to your home?
- If you live in an apartment, can you rent another apartment in the same building?
- Can you rent space nearby to store inventory, files, or other large items that you don't need on a daily basis?
- If you have other people working in your home, can they work from their own homes?

- Would you consider renting a larger apartment or buying a bigger home?

If you really want to move out, then it's time. Simple. Or maybe not quite so simple. Before you go to all the trouble and expense of setting up shop somewhere else, ask yourself this one vital question: Is the problem working from home or is it really owning your own business?

There's nothing to be ashamed of if you decide you don't like running your own business—it's not for everyone. Maybe you're tired of the long hours, or you're not making as much money as you had anticipated, or the lack of security is overwhelming, or maybe you're just plain bored. If any of these are true, it just might be time to polish up your resumé. After all your experience selling for your business, you should have no problem selling yourself to a potential employer.

What are your options if you want to keep the business but move it out of your home? You can go right to renting your own office space or try some intermediate options.

Small business incubators, generally operated by universities, government agencies, and businesses, are designed to nurture new and growing companies. Incubators can provide space (often at below-market rates), shared business services, such as telephone answering, word processing, and secretarial services, as well as access to business equipment like fax and copy machines. Contact the National Business Incubation Association for more information about incubators (see chapter 13, Resources).

Another option is to share office space with others who do the same or similar work. This helps cut down on the cost of rent and other equipment, as well as adding company, moral support, and possibly work-sharing or referral arrangements.

If you're ready to rent your own office but don't want to give up the homey feel, consider renting an office in a home that's been converted to office use. Even if it's not your home, at least it's *a* home! Often many of the original features are retained during conversion.

Another possibility is renting office space in the same neighborhood as your home. The ability to come home for lunch, take work back and forth, and do your errands just might make all the difference.

13 | Resources

Associations

Following is a list of general small business associations. The exact benefits offered by each vary, but most offer networking opportunities; training, seminars, and workshops; a newsletter or magazine; a membership directory; and discounts on business equipment and insurance. Many will also provide funding, in the form of investment and loans, to start or expand your business. In addition, most professions have at least one, and often several, trade associations. To find associations specializing in your area of interest, consult the *Encyclopedia of Associations* (Gale Press), available at most public libraries.

American Association of Professional Consultants
9140 Ward Parkway, Kansas City, MO 64114; (913) 648–2679.
Open to full- and part-time consultants in all fields.

American Consultants League
1290 Palm Avenue, Sarasota, FL 34236; (813) 952–9290.
Open to full- and part-time consultants in all fields.

American Management Association (AMA)
135 W. 50th Street, New York, NY 10020; (212) 903–8270.
International educational organization dedicated to broadening management skills.

Association of Black Women Entrepreneurs (ABWE)
Box 49368, Los Angeles, CA 90049; (213) 624–8639.
National and local chapters for black women entrepreneurs, as well as all other interested women and men.

American Women's Economic Development Corporation (AWED)
71 Vanderbilt Ave., 3rd Floor, New York, NY 10169; (800) 222–AWED.
Nonprofit organization for women business owners and women contemplating business ownership.

National Association for the Self-Employed (NASE)
P.O. Box 612067, Dallas, TX 75261-9968; (800) 232–NASE.
Action-oriented association provides advocacy and lobbying efforts. Provides toll-free business hotline for members.

National Association for Female Executives (NAFE)
P.O. Box 10575, Rockville, MD 20849-9946; (800) 285–NAFE.
National and local chapters for women in business.

National Federation of Independent Business (NFIB)
600 Maryland Ave., SW, Suite 700, Washington, D.C. 20024; (800) NFIB–NOW.
Nonprofit lobbying organization for small and independent businesses.

National Association for Women Business Owners
60 South Federal Street, Suite 400, Chicago, IL 60605; (800) 272–2000.
Local and national chapters for women business owners.

Information Sources

U.S. Small Business Administration (SBA)
National office: 409 Third Street, SW, Washington, D.C. 20416.
Most cities have district offices; check your local phone book under U.S. Government. Economic development agency provides loans, contracts, counseling, training, and other forms of assistance to small businesses. Services include:

The SBA Answer Desk: (800) 827–5722.
Prerecorded information about most aspects of small businesses.

SBA Publications: Low-cost (.50 to $2.00) publications on starting and managing a small business. Request a copy of The Small Business Directory from any local office or write to: Small Business Directory, P.O. Box 1000, Ft. Worth, TX 76119.

Office of Women's Business Ownership: Local chapter services (check your local phone book) include the Women's Network for Entrepreneurial Training (WNET), which matches successful women entrepreneurs with women business owners whose businesses are ready to grow; prebusiness workshops; technical and financial information; conferences, training, and counseling.

Small Business Development Centers: Nationwide university campus-based centers provide management and technical assistance to start-up and existing small businesses.

Service Corps of Retired Executives Association (SCORE): Check the phone book for the local office or call (800) 634-0245. National network of mostly retired volunteer business executives and professionals provide free technical and managerial counseling and training to small businesses.

Small Business Institutes: Students at university centers provide assistance and counseling to small businesses.

Insurance Information Institute
110 William St., New York, NY 10038; (212) 669–9200.
A nonprofit institute that provides basic insurance information. Ask for their current catalog of books, brochures, and videos (prices range from free to $95).

Internal Revenue Service (IRS)
(800) 829–3676.
Publishes free publications of interest to small business owners, including Tax Guide for Small Business, Tax Information on

Partnerships, Tax Information on Corporations, Tax Information on S Corporations. Also sponsors Small Business Tax Workshops.

International Reciprocal Trade Association
9513 Beach Mill Rd., Great Falls, VA 22066. Send an SASE for information about barter exchanges, including a list of barter exchanges near you.

National Association of Small Business Investment Companies (NASBIC)
1199 N. Fairfax Street, Suite 200, Alexandria, VA 22314; (703) 683–1601. For a listing of SBICs (licensed by the US Small Business Administration, they make equity capital and long-term credit available to small businesses), contact the NASBIC for its directory *Venture Capital: Where to Find It.*

National Business Incubation Association
One President St., Athens, OH 45701; (614) 593–4331.
Contact for more information about business incubators and a listing of local incubators.

Magazines

The following magazines are geared specifically to small businesses, home-based businesses, and business owners. Other good sources of information include more general business magazines and newspapers, such as *BusinessWeek, Working Woman,* and the *Wall Street Journal.*

Entrepreneur
2392 Morse Avenue, Irvine, Ca 92714; Subscription information: (800) 274–6229. Monthly magazine with articles on small and medium-sized businesses and franchises. Also publishes small business start-up guides for more than 150 businesses. *Entrepreneurial Woman,* previously published by the same group, has ceased publication.

Home Office Computing
730 Broadway, New York, NY 10003; Subscription information: (800) 678–0118. Geared exclusively to owners of home-based

businesses, this monthly magazine not only covers computers but all aspects of home offices, including time management, budgeting, marketing, etc.

Inc.
38 Commercial Wharf, Boston, MA 02110; Subscription information: (800) 234–0999.
Monthly magazine is geared more to larger companies but sometimes features information applicable to smaller and home-based businesses.

Nation's Business
1615 H Street, NW, Washington, D.C. 20062-2000; Subscription information (800) 727–5869. Published monthly by the United States Chamber of Commerce. Geared to small business owners, including home-based and family businesses.

Success
230 Park Avenue, New York, NY 10169; Subscription information: (800) 234–7324. Monthly magazine for "today's entrepreneurial mind." Geared more to larger business owners, but has some helpful hints and information for home-based businesses.

Your Company
1120 Avenue of the Americas, New York, NY 10036; (212) 382–5792. Quarterly magazine published by American Express Publishing Corporation. Available free to American Express Corporate Cardmembers who are small business owners; others may subscribe for a fee by calling the above number.

Newsletters

Bootstrappin' Entrepreneur
8726 South Sepulveda Blvd., Suite B261, Los Angeles, CA 90045-4082; (310) 568–9861. Quarterly. How-to articles, profiles, and products for people who have started or are interested in starting "micro-enterprises"—small businesses started with $300 to $1,000. The "Freebie Corner" lists free publications, from various sources, of interest to small business owners.

Guerrilla Marketing Newsletter
Guerrilla Marketing International, P.O. Box 1336, Mill Valley, CA 94942; (415) 381–8361. Bimonthly, eight-page newsletter provides advice, research, and techniques on marketing.

National Home Business Report
P.O. Box 2137, Naperville, IL 60567. A quarterly newsletter filled with advice, resources, and information about books and products.

PR INK
594 Broadway, Suite 809, New York, NY 10012. Monthly newsletter with tips and techniques for handling your own public relations.

Win Win Marketing
662 Crestview Dr., San Jose, CA 95117; (800) 292–8625. Bimonthly how-to marketing articles geared to small business owners.

Learning Annex Guides

Check your local bookstore for these other helpful guides from The Learning Annex.

Getting Successfully Published: A Learning Annex Book

Starting Your Own Import-Export Business: A Learning Annex Book

Raising Money in Less than 30 Days: A Learning Annex Book

Unclutter Your Personal Life: A Learning Annex Book

Index

119

Notes

Notes

Notes

Notes

Notes

More Business Books From Carol Publishing Group